50 things you need to know about Heatpumps

A simple guide to renewable heating, but you didn't know who to ask.

Graham Hendra

2022

Dedication

To everyone who has ever thought they were asking me a "stupid question".

There are no stupid questions, its stupid not to ask.

Preface:

I have worked as a technical support engineer in renewable heating for a decade and a half. I specialised in Air source heat pumps in the domestic sector. I joined this industry before it was cool to be in renewable heating and before the government here in the UK jumped on the bandwagon. I have experimented with this technology in my own house, and I am ashamed to say in the early days in our customers houses too. My team and I learnt a lot on the way, we have been cold and wet, we have been shouted at and held high on the shoulders of our peers at times. It's been a real roller coaster.

Over that time, I have been asked literally thousands of questions. I'm inherently lazy so to save me answering them again I chose the most popular questions and tried my best to answer them here. This book is designed to help with the most common questions asked by homeowners and heat pump novices. If it goes down well I might just do one for engineers and heating professionals.

Heat pumps are not really very complicated once you strip away the jargon, so in this book I'm going to try to make the subjects easy to understand using analogies and stories which are easier to relate to. I've tried to keep the answers as simple as I can without wading into thermodynamics and mindless maths.

Hopefully this will be useful to homeowners, installers, energy surveyors and heat pump deniers alike.

I hope you enjoy the results.

Before we start a few things to think about:

How do you heat your house at home?

Does your system run efficiently? When was it last serviced?

How much do you pay for heating per month?

Is that more than your mortgage or rent?

How much do you pay for Sky, mobile phones, WIFI etc per month?

Do you think you pay more than your neighbours for heating? Have you ever checked?

Would you rather go without Sky tv or a hot shower?

If you think about the major items in your house (car, tv, cooker, Wi-Fi, Heating, lights) rate them in order of importance.

If you are honest about these questions, it quickly dawns on you that heating is boring, it's something that happens in the background. We only notice it when it stops working. Heating is not the biggest bill in any household, but it is a significant and growing bill. We in the renewables sector struggle to make this subject sexy, it's because it isn't. No one has ever come to a party at my house and said, "I would love to see your boiler".

A few more questions to think about:

Do you know how much it would cost to have a new boiler installed at home?

How much would a plumber charge to put a new radiator in your lounge?

Most people know that having a radiator installed or replaced would cost a few hundred pounds and having a boiler replaced a few thousand. But in renewables we have failed to let anyone know the price which leaves lots of space for the media to frighten consumers with enormously inflated numbers. A heat pump does not cost £20000 to install unless you are being ripped off or you live in a massive house. Smaller houses cost much less, most average houses, 3 bed semis are average in the UK would be looking at figures much closer to £5k inc vat and would be eligible for the £5k subsidy making £5 k installations realistic. More than a boiler but not much more.

And Lastly

What temperature is your heating system running at? Can you hold the radiators for more than 30 seconds?

When did you last have a bath? How hot do you think the bath was when you got in?

How about a shower?

We have a weird obsession with temperature, most radiators are so hot you can't touch them for more than a few seconds and most of us have the hot water scoldingly hot, so we have to add a splash of cold to make it useable. Its really stupid way to live but we all do it.

In hotels showers are limited to 38 degrees C, you must press a safety button to get hotter than that. A bath is 35degrees C, at 40C you can't get in it without injuring yourself.

In a logical world we would only heat the water to the temperature we needed it at. Adding cold water to scalding hot water to make it useable is like driving the Car with the handbrake on. Madness. We will discuss further.

1 Why are people talking about heat pumps and what problem do they solve?

Everybody has heard of global warming; we all know that the average world temperature has risen over the last couple of hundred years. The major cause is the rise in Carbon Di-Oxide In the atmosphere from burning fossil fuels. Before the rise in CO2 and the heat from the sun balanced with the amount of heat leaving the earth so the temperature remained stable, Carbon Di-oxide acts like a blanket or duvet over the earth trapping the heat so it can't escape as quickly so the world slowly warms up.

Before we released this CO2 into the atmosphere it was buried deep in the ground as Oil, Gas and Coal for millions of years. The coal was made up of plant waste and the oil and gas from sea creatures mostly plankton and algae, not dinosaurs and fish as most people think. We have been digging coal, gas and Oil up for a few hundred years slowly re-releasing the CO2 back into the atmosphere again.

We all have to take responsibility for our Carbon emissions and try to reduce them, this means burning less fuel in your car, in the stuff you buy and consume and of course from your house. Your home heating is one of the biggest fuel consumers you own, but it's hidden in a cupboard, so no one thinks about it.

When did you last see your boiler?

A heat pump is just a low carbon boiler (replacement) which emits under half the Carbon dioxide of a gas or Oil boiler, so it's a good place to look if you want to reduce your carbon output. It's not perfect but it's a great place to start.

In the UK 22 million houses have central heating, 85% of those houses use gas.

Between April 2020 and April 2021 1.75 million boilers were sold in the UK. 1.4 million of those were gas combi boilers. You probably have a gas combi boiler at home? In the same period (1 year) only 70 thousand heat pumps were sold.

In 2021 1 in 25 heating systems sold was a heat pump. If this was a school report it would say, "must try harder"

Discussion points:

Every day 192 heat pumps and 4794 gas boilers are installed in the UK, why so few heat pumps- Are they too expensive?

Are they not very good after all?

Be honest when did you first hear about heat pumps?

Have you ever seen a heat pump?

Have you got a heat pump at home?

Heat pumps are not very well known our industry has not been very good or successful at promoting them and their benefits. There have been incentives, but they were complex and not widely known. Since 2021 the government and the press have promoted the technology more and the industry has grown significantly since then. There is a significant backlash against the technology as there always is with anything new, but these arguments will fade away as heat pumps become more widespread.

2 What is a heat pump?

A heat pump is a machine which is used to heat your house and hot water, it's quite simply just an alternative to a conventional fossil fuel boiler. Its heats water which is pumped around your house using the copper pipes and warms your radiators or underfloor heating.

Think of It as a boiler which is designed to replace your gas or oil boiler with a much greener renewable, low carbon alternative. Heat pumps are often called renewable boilers.

The biggest difference between a boiler and a heat pump is your Heat pump is going to live outside in the garden, it needs to go outside because it's going to capture most of the heat from the air.

Just like in your boiler the pipes connect to the heat pump, we call them flow and return instead of out and in. You can see them on the bottom left of this unit here.

3 How does a conventional heating system work and what does it look like?

22 million houses in the UK have a central heating system of which most have gas boilers.

Gas boilers tend to be white boxes hidden in kitchen cupboards. Like this.

Inside your boiler

there is a gas burner which burns the gas, it's just like a giant gas hob, it warms up the pipes containing the water, this is pumped around the house to heat the radiators.

Your house will have a network of pipes running around taking the water from the boiler to each of the radiators, under floor heating loops and hot water cylinder.

Think of your boiler as a pan of hot water on the stove, the boiler warms the water and pumps it around the house. It's a very simple machine.

Typically, a gas hob ring is 3kW, similar in power to a kettle. Think about it how long does it take to boil a kettle? It takes a similar time to boil a pan of spuds on the hob.

Your boiler is often the equivalent of 10 kettles or gas rings, it needs to be to warm the water quickly, no one wants to wait 5 minutes to get in the shower.

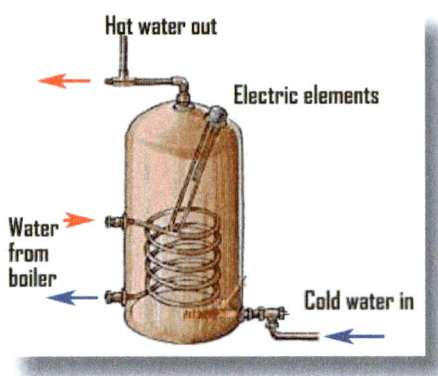

From the 1960s to the 1990s most people had gas boilers with a copper hot water cylinder in an airing cupboard. The cylinder often was covered in a red jacket.

In the 1990s the combi boiler came along, it has been very successful, the advantage with the combi was you don't have a hot water cylinder, the boiler instantly heats the cold water from the mains up to toasty warm as you use it. It's an instant gas water heater. With a combi it takes a while for the water to come out of the taps warm. You must get the boiler burners going then heat the water.

In larger houses people still use hot water cylinders. If you have a boiler and a hot water cylinder your heating engineer will call this a system boiler, system boilers often have a smaller heat output, they don't have to be as big, they don't have to provide

instant hot water. They can take their time heating the cylinder and storing it ready for you to take a shower anytime.
The hot water cylinder is just a big bucket of water with insulation around it. Years ago, it used to be copper and wrapped in a red duvet, now they are stainless steel with expanded foam insulation.

If you have an oil or LPG boiler it's just the same, but the fuel for the flame is different and comes from a storage tank in the garden.

4 How does a heat pump work?

I'm sure you have a freezer at home, I have a SMEG because I think the name is funny, I liked Red Dwarf.

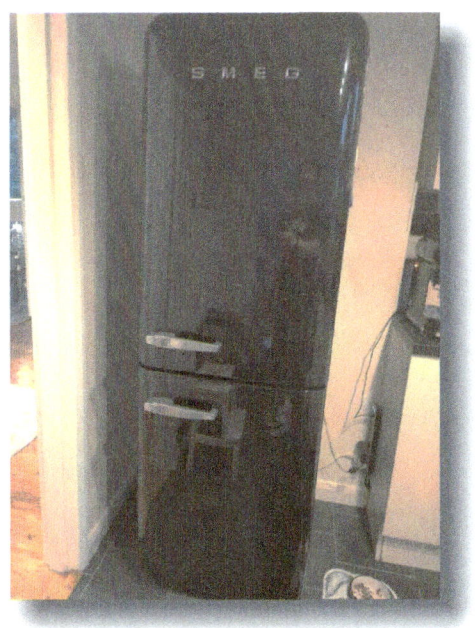

My freezer is amazing, I can take some hot cross buns, put them inside, close the door and a few hours later they are frozen solid. Contrary to popular belief there is nothing magic going on here.

Inside the freezer under all that ice there are some silver tubes, inside the tubes is a refrigerant, its nothing fancy, my freezer uses a refrigerant called propane, heat pump geeks call it R290, it's the stuff you use to fuel your barbeque. You can buy it in B and Q.

All Refrigerants have one amazing quality, they can absorb enormous amounts of heat and can be moved around efficiently. In my freezer the propane is very cold, it literally sucks the heat out of anything near it, in my case those hot cross buns. Hot goes to cold.

The refrigerant is moved around the freezer using a pump, it's the buzzy thing that looks like a black football on the back. It's quite literally an electrically driven pump, we fridge engineers think we are clever, so we call it a compressor, it's a pump.

The pump sucks in the cold refrigerant (now full of hot cross bun heat) and compresses it, compressing it is a bit like wringing out a sponge. The heat is squeezed out of the refrigerant as its pumped through the black coil on the back of my freezer, where the heat is dumped into my kitchen. Once the refrigerant has cooled off it returns through a valve very like the one you see on the end of your radiator, but much smaller. As the refrigerant goes through the valve the pressure drops and so does the temperature, so It enters the freezer at low temperature ready to capture

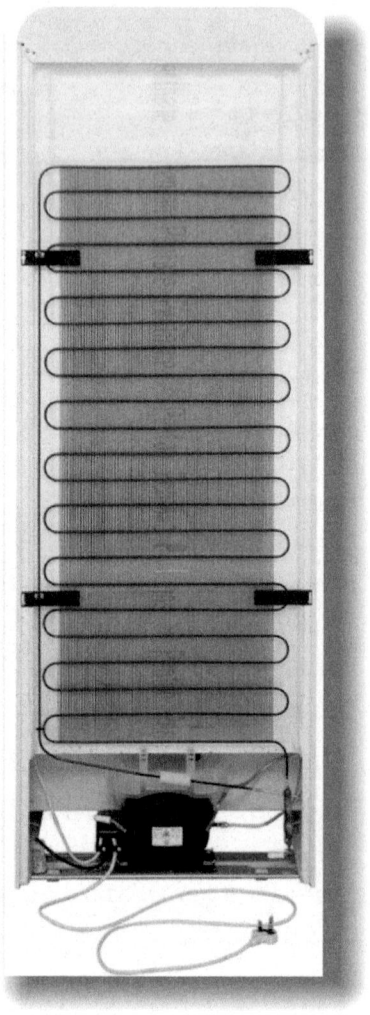

some more heat from my food. The refrigerant is never used up, it just goes round and round again and again.

To recap, I suck heat out of my hot cross buns and dump the heat into my kitchen. I'm quite literally heating my kitchen with a combination of electrical power and heat from my food. So, it shouldn't be called a freezer it's a food to kitchen heat pump.

So what? What's this got to do with heat pumps? Simple.

DO NOT TRY THIS AT HOME, if I took my freezer outside and ripped the doors off it would now cool down the air in the garden instead of the food inside, the heat from the air would get sucked into the refrigerant, (remember hot goes to cold) the refrigerant would go through the pump, get squeezed and the heat would be discharged out of the back of the freezer using the black coil here.

If I was to drizzle water over the black coil at the back of the freezer and collect it at the bottom it would be lovely and warm, I could run inside with the bucket and pour it through my radiators.

This is exactly how your air source heat pump works; it is a freezer in the garden and a coil heating water. That is quite literally all there is too it.

An air source heat pumps is a massive freezer which cools the garden and heats water, you don't even need a bucket, we do that bit for you too. There is nothing new in this technology, I have had a freezer since I was a kid. My freezer has been running for 11 years at a constant -19 degrees C. It's never been maintained, it's never broken down, it just goes on and on and on.

Heat pumps are also not new technology, they are simple machines using freezer technology that everyone knows, works, you have one at home already.

It amazes me that people say heat pumps don't work in the cold and are unreliable. My freezer is cold every day and is completely reliable. Its exactly the same technology as a heat pump.

5 Is a heat pump Noisy?

To heat your water, we suck the heat out of the air in the garden. Air holds a lot less heat than water, so you have capture the heat from a lot of air to warm the water up.

A 16 kW Samsung unit sucks 100 m^3 of air through it every minute. A hair dryer moves 70m^3 of air every hour. The heat pump moves 85 times more air. To put these figures into conceivable units, this heat pump moves all the air inside a 40-foot HGV lorry trailer every 40 seconds.

Moving air quickly is noisy, see hairdryer above. Moving air slowly is quiet, think of roof fans in restaurants.

The manufacturers must decide whether to make the heat pumps small and noisy with fast moving air or big and quiet with slower moving air. There is a happy medium

A heat pump is a big box, here is me next to a 16kW Samsung unit. A Midea or Mitsubishi 14kW is half the height but a bit fatter.

Most manufacturers measure the noise of the unit in dB or decibels, but this doesn't mean much to anyone but acoustic engineers.

How many decibels is the noise in this room? You can only guess unless you have a sound meter. It's complicated by the fact that sound scales are not linear or equal. 60dB is half as loud as 63dB. So, me telling you a unit is 58 dB doesn't mean a lot.

A heat pump noise output varies as the output goes up, when working gently on a Spring or Autumn Day they are very quiet, you have to approach the unit and listen carefully to hear them running. When they are flat out on a cold day, and they are covered in ice they are much louder. Think of a large desk fan and a microwave oven both running together. That's the noise a heat pump will make at its noisiest, you can even try this at home before you buy a heat pump to see what it's like.

Is that too noisy for you? Only you can answer this question

6 Is a heat pump cheaper to run than a boiler?

Yes, but only a bit if we are comparing it with a brand-new mains gas boiler. Ok let's expand on that,

Heat is measured in kilo Watt hours, shortened to kWhrs. 1 kWhr is one kilo Watt for 1 hour.

A 3kW electric blower fire draws 3kW. If I leave it on for 1 hour, it will use 3kW hours of electricity.

Today in May 2022 a kWhr of gas costs me 7.5 pence

If we assume the boiler, we burn it in is 90% efficient we need to burn more than 1 kWhr of gas to get 1 kWhr of heat.

The formula is 7.5 Pence / 0.9 (90% is 0.9) = 8.3 pence.

With a gas boiler a unit of heat 1 kWhr costs 8.3 Pence, 3kWhrs of energy would cost 25 pence.

The electric blower fire above uses electricity, today in December 2021 a kWhr of gas costs me 30 pence. If we assume the electric heater is 100% efficient, we use 1 kWhr of electricity to get 1 kWhr of heat.

With an electric heater a unit of heat 1 kWhr costs 30 Pence, 3 kWhrs would cost 90 pence.

A heat pump also uses electricity, but for every 1 kWhr of electricity used it captures 2 free KWhrs of heat from the garden. The bit from the garden is free and renewable.

Today in December 2021 a kWhr of electricity costs me 30 pence

The heat pump will use 1kWhr of electricity and add it to 2 free units of energy, so we use 1 kWhr of electricity to get 3 kWhr of heat.

With a heat pump a unit of heat 1 kWhr costs 30 Pence / 3 = 10 Pence, 3kWhrs cost 30 pence.

To recap, 3 kWhrs of heat costs:

25 Pence with Gas, 90 Pence with an electric heater and 30 Pence with a heat pump.

Assuming the gas and electricity prices don't change, a heat pump is 20% more expensive than a gas boiler.

But if your boiler is old, it won't be 90% efficient so it will cost more to provide a kWhr of heat and if we can make the heat pump capture more than 2 units of heat from the garden, we can reduce its run cost. This is the aim of the system designer.

If the heat pump captured 3 free units of heat for every kWhr of electricity used, would it be cheaper or more expensive to run?

If the electricity price fell would a heat pump be cheaper than a gas boiler?

If someone has a very cheap tariff for electricity of 10p per kWhr and you gather 2 free units of heat from the garden how much would a kWhr of heat cost?

If electric heaters are so expensive to run, why do we use them in social housing?

My new kettle is 2kW and electric costs 30 Pence per kWhr. How much does my kettle cost to run for 1 hour, ½ an hour?

If the heat pump captured 3 free units of heat for every kWhr of electricity used, would it be cheaper or more expensive to run? Cheaper it would now use 1kWhr of electricity at 30 pence and make 4 units of heat so that's 7.5p / kWhr.

If the electricity price fell would a heat pump be cheaper than a gas boiler? Yes, but only if the gas price didn't fall too.

If someone has a very cheap tariff for electricity of 10p per kWhr and you gather 2 free units of heat from the garden how much would a kWhr of heat cost? If I put 1 kWhr of electricity in and captured 2 free from the garden then 3 kWhrs would cost 0 pence, 1 kWhr would cost 3.33 pence.

If electric heaters are so expensive to run, why do we use them in social housing? Good question, electric heaters are cheap to install but horribly expensive to run. The installer and builder are happy, the homeowner is not. Installing Direct electric heating is immoral in low-income households.

My new kettle is 2kW and electric costs 30 Pence per kWhr. How much does my kettle cost to run for 1 hour, ½ an hour? 2kWhrs is 60 pence, I use 2 kWhrs in one hour or 1 kWhr in half an hour so 30 pence.

7 Is a heat pump more efficient than a boiler and what is COP?

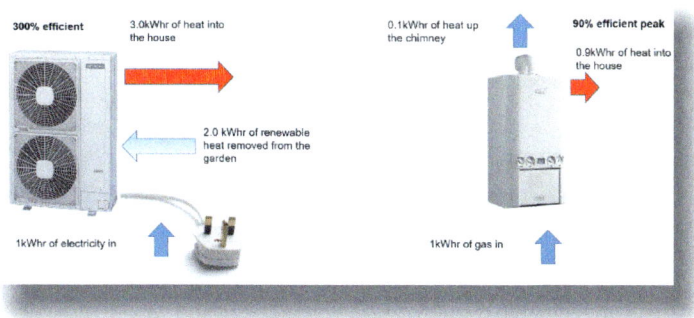

Most brand-new gas boilers are advertised as 90 % efficient, so for every 1kWhr of gas we burn in the boiler we get 0.9kWhrs of heat into the building and 0.1kWhr as waste heat goes up the chimney. Boiler engineers call the chimney a flue.

According to OFGEM, boiler efficiency has risen over the last few years, a 10-year-old boiler is likely to be 83% efficient.

In the world of Heat pumps, for every 1kWhr of electricity used to drive the compressor, it harvests 2 kWhrs of heat from the air in the garden. The result is 3 kWhrs of heat go into the house. So, we would say 1 in, 3 out, that is the same as 300% efficient.

However, it sounds strange to say anything is over 100% efficient, it's not what people are used to hearing. When we are talking about heat pump performance, we divide the 300% by 100 to make 3. We say the heat pump has a coefficient of Performance or COP of 3.

Coefficient of performance is just percentage efficiency divided by 100.

A boiler has a COP of 0.9, a heat pump has a COP of 3

Heat pumps are always more efficient than boilers.

What's the COP of an electric blower fire?

What's the COP of a television?

Every electrical device is 100% efficient as a heater, all the energy ends up as heat in the room. Example you use 200Watts to operate the television, all 200 Watts end up in the room as heat. the COP is 1.

If you want to be pedantic, tumble driers are 100% efficient but because they blow the warm wet air outside not all the heat ends up in the building so strictly, they are not 100% efficient heaters. But you shouldn't have a tumble drier anyhow, it is an ecological disaster. Use a washing line its much greener and cheaper.

8 What temperature does a heat pump or boiler work at and what effect does that have in the house?

If you live in a house with a gas, oil, or LPG boiler its very common that it will be set up to run with radiators of 70 degrees centigrade. 70 degrees is very hot to the touch, you can touch the radiator without getting scalded, but you cannot hold the radiator tight for more than a few seconds.

It is possible to run the temperature lower than this with a boiler, there is usually a knob or some buttons on the front which allow you to adjust it but most systems are set up very hot.

In the example below we have set the boiler to send water into the system at 75 degrees C. The water moves slowly through the radiator, so it has a lot of time to lose its heat into the room. The water leaves the radiator at 65 degrees C. The average radiator temperature is between 75 as the water enters and 65 C as the water leaves, in this example the radiator is 70 degrees C average temperature.

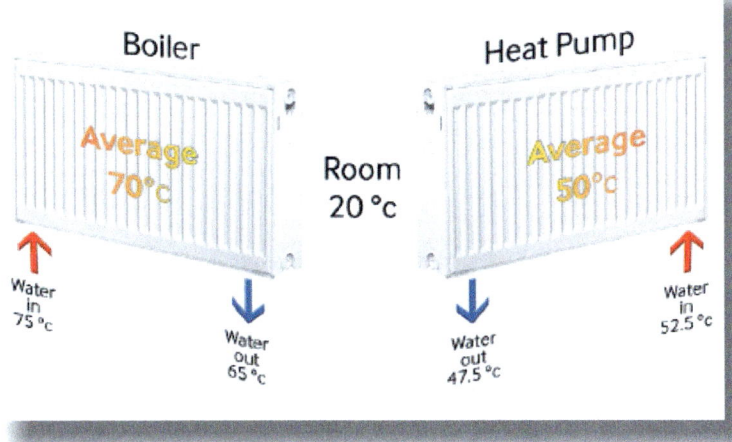

In a heating system using a heat pump there are 2 main differences:

The first is that the run cost of any heat pump rises as the water temperature rises. Another way of looking at this is as the water temperature goes up the efficiency falls. We try to run the heat pump a lower temperature so the homeowner experiences greater savings.
The second difference is we move the water very quickly through the heating system and radiators, this is again to increase the efficiency of the heat pump and reduce the run costs.

Most heat pumps send water out to the radiators at 52.5C, we move the water very quickly through the radiator, so it has less time to lose its heat. It leaves the radiator only 5 degrees colder at 47.5C. The average radiator temperature is between 52.5 and 47.5C so it's 50 degrees C.

A radiator at 50 degrees C is nice and warm to the touch, you can hold it with your hands for a few minutes without scalding.

So, heat pumps are set to run radiators at lower temperatures, it still means the house is warm but it can take longer to get up to temperature if you turn it off. We like to keep heat pumps running all the time maintaining the house at a steady temperature. Its cheaper than time clocking the heat pump and letting the house cool down.

9 Do I need special radiators or underfloor heating when using a heat pump? And why are the radiators so big?

In Q 8 we discussed the temperatures in a heating system.

Underfloor heating is normally designed to run at much lower temperatures than radiators, it's not unusual for the underfloor heating to run at between 35- and 45-degrees C. Remember with underfloor heating you must be able to comfortably stand on the warm floor for long periods of time. If the underfloor heating was the same temperature as a radiator, you would be hopping from foot to foot.

If we are replacing a boiler with a heat pump and connecting it to underfloor heating its both easy and efficient for us to run the heat pump at exactly the same temperature the boiler was running at, 35-45 degrees C. People say underfloor heating is ideal for a heat pump, its ideal because it's simple to do.

With radiators it's a little more complicated. In a gas boiler heating system, you typically run the radiators at 70 degrees C, in a heat pump you run radiators at 50 degrees C. There is no difference between the radiators used for a boiler or a heat pump, all radiators will work on both systems.

The amount of heat a radiator gives out is determined by its temperature. If the radiator is exactly the same temperature as your room, it won't heat up the room at all. The hotter the radiator is the more heat it gives out and the quicker it can heat the room up.

If I disconnect a boiler from a radiator and connect a heat pump, the radiator will still work, but the amount of heat coming out of the radiator will fall because the radiator is colder. The solution is to either raise the temperature of the water from the heat pump, (this is very hard to do in 2022 but watch this space and it raises the run cost) or make the radiator

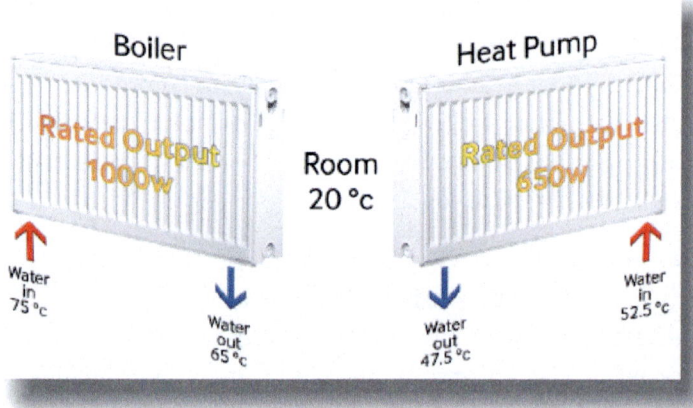

larger.

In the example above the same radiator is used, on the left connected to a boiler it gives out 1000 Watts or 1kW of heat. If the same radiator is connected to a heat pump it only gives out 650 Watts or 0.65kW.

In most cases when we are retrofitting a heat pump to a gas boiler heating system, we must change from a single panel radiator to a double panel radiator to increase the size and output of the radiator.

When the heat loss and heat pump survey is completed, the surveyors measure the radiator size to work out which radiators need upgrading or changing when a heat pump is connected. It is very difficult to tell if the radiator will be big enough just by looking.

rad maths	w/m^2
towel	320
single panel	640
single convector	850
double Panel	1121
double convector	**1480**

As a really rough guide we can measure the size of your radiator and calculate its output using this table. A 1000mm x 500mm radiator is 0.5 metres square.

If it was running at 50C and a room temperature of 20C the output would be 1480 / 2 = 740 Watts if it's a double convector.

10 Can you buy a high temperature heat pump? And is it expensive to run?

Most heat pumps available today operate up to 50 or 55 degrees C, these include:

Daikin Mitsubishi, Vaillant, Midea, Samsung etc. However, there

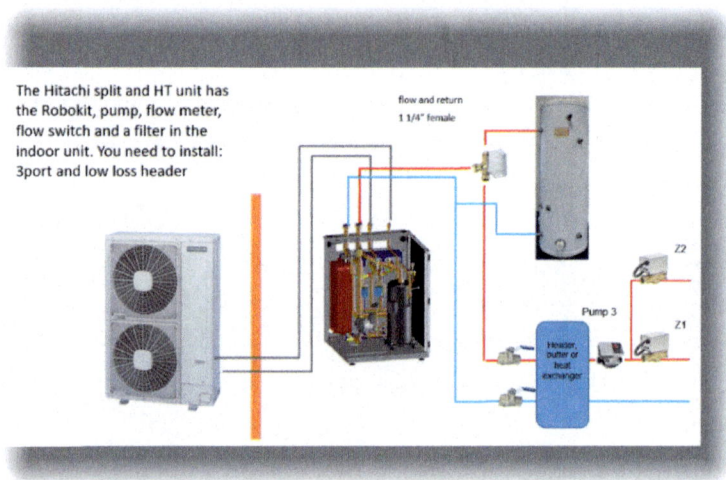

are a few high temperature heat pumps available.

In heat pumps anything over 65 degrees C is high temperature. It's very important to check that the manufacturer is not fibbing to you, they are addicted to giving up meaningless data. Many heat pumps can get to 65C but only if it's warm, above 10 degrees C outside. You want proof that your chosen unit will run at 65C when its cold outside, check the figures at -5C ambient.

At time of writing May 2022 there are only a handful of true high temperature units available on the market which can reach 65C when its cold outside. These include Daikin Atherma 3 HT 65 degrees C and Hitachi S80 HT 80 degrees C.

High temperature heat pumps are more expensive to build and therefore to buy, they are high performance machines and they

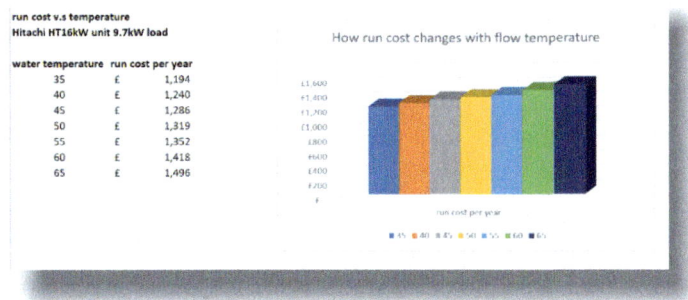

cost more to run see below.

For example, in an average 120m square, 3-bedroom house with a 9.7kW load:

If I change the radiators and run them at 50 C with a low temperature heat pump the run cost will be £1319 per year.

If I run the radiators at 65 degrees C using a high temperature heat pump the run cost will rise to £1496 a year an increase of £177 or 15% a year.

The run cost rises, the efficiency falls and so does the carbon saving.

Note high temperature heat pumps are designed to run at these higher temperatures. Low temperature heat pumps are designed to work well in the 40-50 degrees C range. Pushing a low temperature heat pump to run at 60 degrees can make the run cost rise very dramatically.

If you need to go for a high temperature solution because you can't or wont change the radiators, pipework or hot water cylinder make sure you choose the appropriate machine.

In 2023 we will see an influx in higher temperature heat pumps using propane or R290 as a refrigerant. These are designed to simply replace your boiler with the minimum of fuss.

11 Do I have to have a hot water cylinder?

Most gas central heating systems are combi boilers, they heat the water for your bath and shower instantly. This is one of the appeals of the combi boiler, you only heat the water as you need it and you don't have to have a cylinder cupboard.

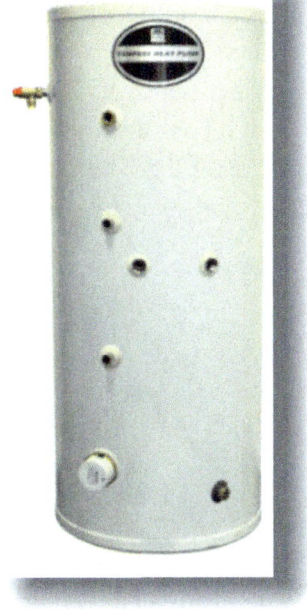

With a system boiler you have a smaller boiler and a hot water cylinder, think of it as a hot water battery, you charge it up with hot water and use it when you need it.

With a heat pump we are not able to heat the water up quickly enough to make instant hot water. Heat pumps also have a start-up cycle which means it can take up to 5 minutes before the unit runs flat out. Now imagine being in the shower waiting for 5 minutes for the heat pump to wind up and produce your hot water. No one would want to do this. There are and never will be combi heat pumps.

The solution is to use the heat pump to heat up a hot water cylinder just like we do with a system boiler. The heat pump will take about an hour to heat the cylinder from cold. We size the cylinder to suit the house.

The formula to work out the cylinder size is simple; first work out how many people live in the house, we allow 1 person per bedroom plus 1. So, for a 3 bed house we allow 4 people. Each person uses between 45 and 55 litres of hot water per day.

4 people = 200 litres of hot water so we would recommend a 200l cylinder.

Cylinders come in 200, 250,300,400,500 and then custom sizes.

There is nothing wrong with putting in a larger hot water cylinder except its bigger, more expensive to buy (about £200 more expensive as you go up one size) and it takes longer to heat it back up. Think of it like a kettle, if its half full it will heat up faster than if its full to the top. The more water in the kettle the more time (and energy) it takes.

What is wrong with putting in a too small cylinder?

If I have a 4-bed house but I live alone, what size cylinder would you recommend?

If the cylinder is too small you will keep running out of hot water, it's very irritating.

If you live alone in a big 4 bed house, we recommend the correct size cylinder for the house so when guests come or when you sell it you don't have to up size the cylinder, but its your house, you get to decide.

12 Why can't I keep my old cylinder?

The water which goes through the heat pump or boiler and the radiators is not clean, it has chemicals called inhibitors in it to stop corrosion, the water that comes out your taps does not go through the heat pump. The water in the cylinder is heated using a coil, the coil has the heat pump or boiler water in it. So, the heat pump or boiler heats the water indirectly.

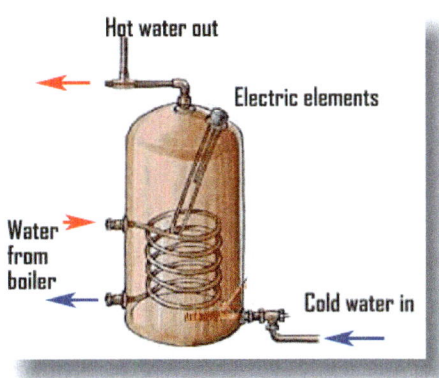

Inside the cylinder is your warm water for your taps, cold water from the mains comes in at the bottom and pushes the hot water out of the top.

When you buy a basic hot water cylinder for a boiler it has a small coil inside, we measure the coil size in units of area, metres Squared, m^2. It's not uncommon for a standard cylinder to have a coil of 1m^2. This is ok with a boiler because the boiler runs at high temperature 75C making a small coil acceptable.

In a heat pump cylinder, everything is the same except the coil is 3 times bigger, we typically have a 3m^2 coil. Like this one here, note how its made up of 3 coils connected together. We use the big coil because we run the heat pump at lower temperatures 55C.

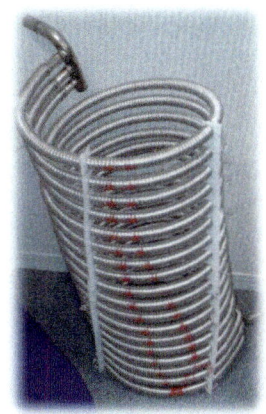

The larger coil area is used to reduce the time we need to heat the cylinder up.

This is a graph showing the heat up time, we call it the recovery

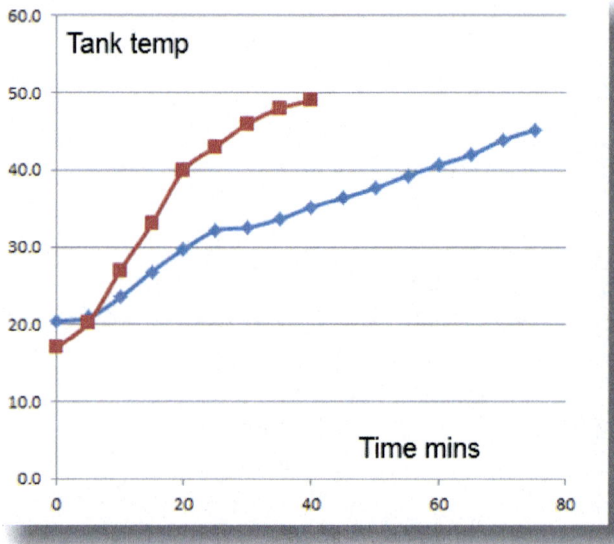

time, of my 180Litre cylinder at home using a heat pump. In blue it shows how long it took to heat my old tank designed for a boiler with a 1m coil. In red it shows the time required using my new tank with a 3m coil.

With a heat pump we like to heat the hot water as quickly as possible, we cannot heat the house and the hot water cylinder at the same time so we get in, heat the cylinder quickly and get back to heating the house before anyone notices. Every minute spent heating the cylinder is a minute I'm not heating the house.

Technically you could connect your old hot water cylinder to a heat pump, but it would take so long to heat up it would leave the house cold.

When high temperature heat pumps which can operate at the same temperature as your old boiler become mainstream you won't need to change your hot water cylinder if it works well and is still in good condition.

13 Do heat pumps have to be next to the house or can they go down the garden?

Your heat pump is going to replace your boiler, for ease of installation putting it as close to the existing boiler as you can is the simplest solution.

Most of the units used in the UK are Monoblock heat pumps. Monoblock's have the advantage that everything comes in one box, think of them as outdoor mounted boilers. A Monoblock heat pump is connected to the water pipework in place of a boiler. The heating engineer has to get the pipes from where the boiler used to be, to where the new heat pump is going. We also need to push the water from the heat pump, into the house, around the radiators and back out again using a water pump. The further you have to push the bigger the pumps need

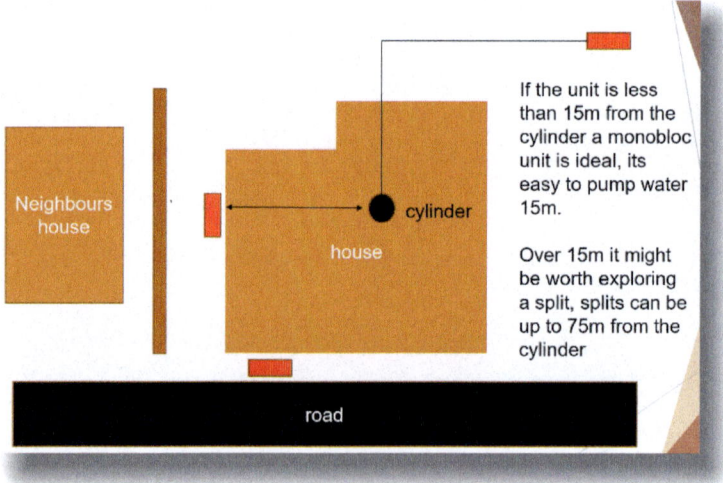

to be.

As a rule, we recommend the monobloc heat pump is no further than 15 metres from the hot water cylinder.

It is possible to run a monobloc unit more than 15 metres, but we have to make the pipework bigger diameter, or we need to increase the pump size. Some Monobloc heat pumps have the pump inside, Midea Panasonic Daikin etc, it's very difficult to increase the pump size. Some the pump is external, Samsung Mitsubishi etc so it's simple to upgrade.

If the customer wants the pipework buried or hidden, it can be very expensive, we tell them it costs £100 a metre if they want to do this.

There are special units called Splits which are designed when the customer wants the unit more then 20M away from the house, we will discuss them later.

14 Heat pumps are ugly, can I put them inside?

NO!

Heat pumps consume huge amounts of air. If you put a heat pump in a single garage it would use all the air every 15 seconds, very quickly the garage would become very cold.

Likewise, your loft, it might be warm up there on sunny days but it won't be on cold November evenings. A 16 kW Samsung unit sucks 100 m^3 of air through it every minute. To put these figures into conceivable units, this heat pump moves all the air inside a 40-foot HGV lorry trailer every 40 seconds.

It is not possible to put the unit inside in ANY circumstances. It wants to be in a position where it can get hold of limitless quantities of fresh air.

15 Can I put a trellis over it?

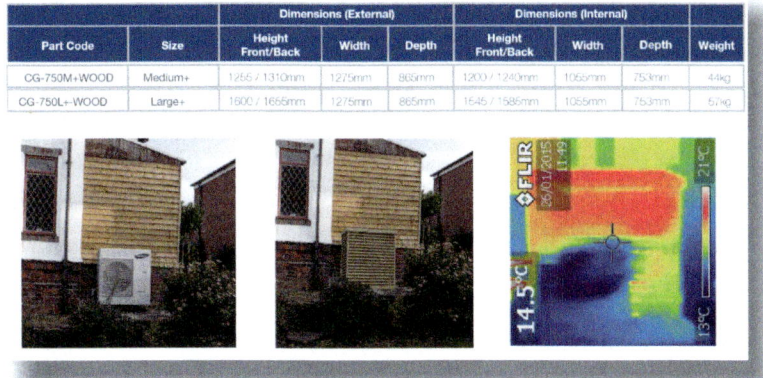

Part Code	Size	Dimensions (External)			Dimensions (Internal)			Weight
		Height Front/Back	Width	Depth	Height Front/Back	Width	Depth	
CG-750M+WOOD	Medium+	1255 / 1310mm	1275mm	865mm	1200 / 1240mm	1055mm	753mm	44kg
CG-750L+WOOD	Large+	1600 / 1655mm	1275mm	865mm	1545 / 1585mm	1055mm	753mm	57kg

If you want to cover the heat pump up you have to do it allowing for the airflow through the unit. Making a cover yourself or putting a trellis in front of it is not a good idea. Restricting the airflow causes high run cost and poor efficiency. The units work best if they are out in the open.

The most important thing to consider is that as the air goes through your heat pump we suck the heat out of the air, so it leaves 10 degrees C colder than it enters, the now very cold air that is blown out the front needs to get discharged into the garden, we don't want it going through the unit again.

If you restrict the air flow and make the air recirculate thorough the unit more than once you can see the unit freezing up and the run cost rising.

Specialist enclosures can be used if they have been tested and don't affect the airflow.

16 How long will a boiler or heat pump last?

Boilers are designed to last 10-15 years

Some last much longer than that and are still going long after their expected life span, some fail in a shorter rime. A lot depends on how you use them and if they are abused.

Heat pumps are the same, they are designed to last 10-15 years, some will last less, some more.

I have an air sourced heat pump in my office which is now 13 years old, it still works well.

Heat pumps are based on air conditioning units, it's common for air conditioning units to still be running 10-20 years after they are installed if they are looked after and well installed to begin with.

When I am asked the life of a heat pump I say 11 years 8 months, its sounds like someone measured it but it's completely made up.

17 People say heat pumps don't work, is this true?

Discuss:

If heat pumps didn't work, what do you think would happen in Winter?

How long do you think the technology would last with a bad reputation?

It's true if you type bad heat pump in google you can find bad examples, do you think this is poor equipment or poor installation of good equipment?

It's highly unlikely that any manufacturer would sell a product that didn't work. Heat pumps are an applied technology, this means that they are only a small part of the heating system. To get the heating to work well you need to wire and pipe it up correctly and make sure the whole system of pipe and radiators all work together. If any part of the system doesn't work the consumer will point to the heat pump. The heat pump is the only part of the system what has a manufacturers name on it. No one ever blames the radiator manufacturer or the pipe work supplier.

It's very important that the system designer gets everything sized correctly and that the installer puts it in exactly as designed. The commissioning engineer is there to test it all work correctly.

In the bad old days, there were no rules about how to size the kit, it was a bit of a wild West. When MCS came along with the RHI grants in 2013 they set out strict procedures explaining how we size and choose a heat pump. This has insured that the units are sized and specified correctly.

Saying a heat pump doesn't work is as ridiculous as saying electric cars don't work. Idiots still say electric cars are like milk floats, the same idiots say heat pumps don't work as they reach for the frozen pizza out of the freezer.

The biggest challenge is it's a bit harder to specify a heat pump than a boiler, some people fear the technology. Saying it doesn't work is just them admitting they don't understand, maybe they should read this book.

18 Will heat pumps get more efficient, prettier, or cheaper in the next 5 years?

Heat pump design has not changed significantly over the last 15 years. The problem we are faced with is the amount of air we must move remains a constant, it can't be changed. If we make the units small, they will be noisy as the air will move quickly. You can't have small and quiet.

In 2010 a 9kW unit looked like this:

In 2022 it looked like this

There are moves towards short fat units, in the past we used to use tall double fan very tall so-called tombstone units but these are falling out of favour nowadays.

The efficiency of the units has not changed significantly either, but the output temperatures have risen from 50 to 60 degrees C and the refrigerants used in the units are much greener. It is predicted that heat pumps will become cheaper over time but over the last 10 years this has not been the case.

	Capacity -2/50	Energy in	COP	max temperature
2012	11.3	5.7	1.98	48C
2015	11.42	6.60	1.79	50C
2021	12.28	6.86	1.79	60C

19 Will I be cold in winter? Heat pumps don't work when it's cold.

When we specify a heat pump for your house, we follow a very strict set of guidelines laid out by MCS. MCS are the gatekeepers to the governments Grants. If you want a grant you have to follow the procedures.

Heat pump surveyors measure ever room in your house noting what the house is constructed from and what insulation you have. We design a system that can heat every room of the house to a set temperature, typically 21 degrees C, in every room of the house on the coldest day of the year as detailed by MCS below.

design ambient temperatures	air temp	ground temp	altitude m
Plymouth	0.20	11	27
Belfast	-1.20	10.5	68
Cardiff	-1.60	9.9	67
London	-1.80	10.2	25
Manchester	-2.20	10	75
Birmingham	-3.40	9.8	96
Edinburgh	-3.40	8.5	35
Glasgow	-3.90	8.5	5
Channel Islands	-0.20	11	0

MCS have worked out the temperature we should design too, they have calculated that the temperature is above these levels for 99% of the year. On a few days of the year for a couple of hours the temperature may fall below these levels, but its considered wasteful to design a system for these rare occurrences.

We complete a full heat load report on the house and then plot what your house needs vs. the output of the chosen heat pump.

Like below:

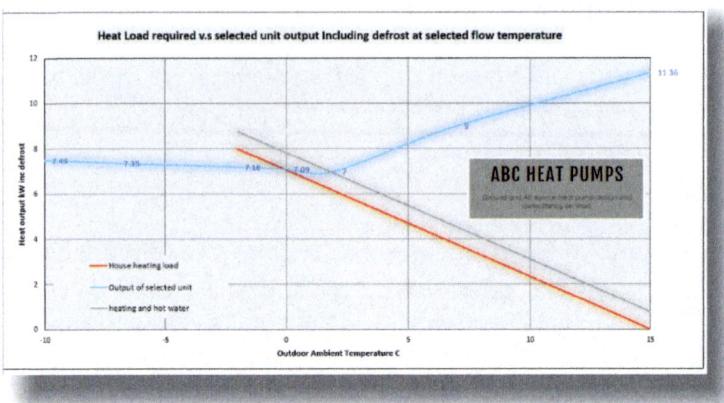

Note the Red line is the heating demand, and the Grey is the heating plus the hot water demand. The Blue shows the amount of heat the chosen heat pump can give. In this case this machine would fail the MCS test, it's not big enough. Note how the unit will only maintain the design room temperature if its above 0 degrees C outside. This is not good enough so we cannot install this unit. All installers will provide you with a graph like this to show you that the unit is capable of doing the job.

> Discuss:
>
> If a unit is not big enough, what do you think will happen in the house?
>
> If the unit is too big for the job what will happen?
>
> If the customer wants room temperatures of 23 degrees C would you use a bigger or smaller heat pump?

I look at is as the size of the unit determines how many degrees hotter than the outside air can the heat pump keep the rooms in the house. In London we design for a room temperature of 21C when its -2 outside. That means the heat pump should be able to hold the house 23 degrees above the air temperature.

If the heat pump is too small it might only be able to hold the house 18 degrees Above the air temperature, so if its 0 outside the house will only be at 18C. If the heat pump is too big it might be able to hold the house 25 degrees above air temperature so even when its -2 outside, you can still have 23 degrees C in every room. Its your house, tell the system designer what temperature you want, and they will calculate this for you.

If we choose the next size up heat pump you can see the unit is

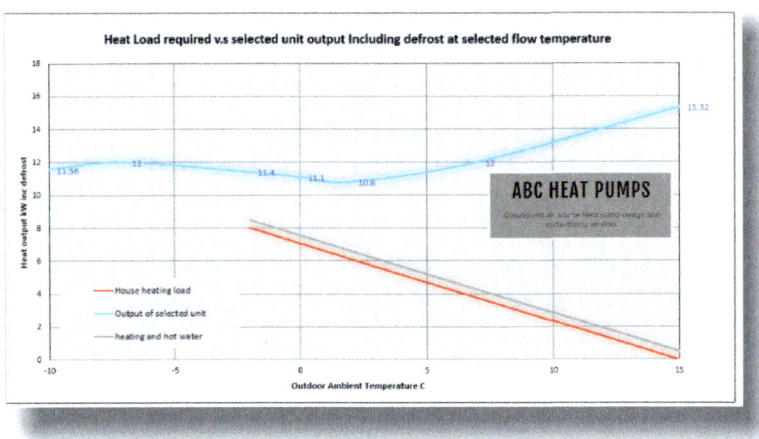

easily able to cope with the load.

MCS encourage us to oversize the unit to make sure you are not cold. The ONLY disadvantage of oversizing is the unit is more expensive to buy. All heat pumps modulate their outputs to meet the demand of the house so buying a larger unit means it will very rarely go flat out.

20 Will a heat pump work when its cold outside?

We had minus 25 C last winter.

It is very common for people to exaggerate just how cold it was last year, here are the actual temperatures from the web. It is possible to get this information very easily.

But if the customer is really worried let's look at the output figures for the heat pump.

In every house as it gets colder outside the amount of heat we need goes up. Like this in Red:

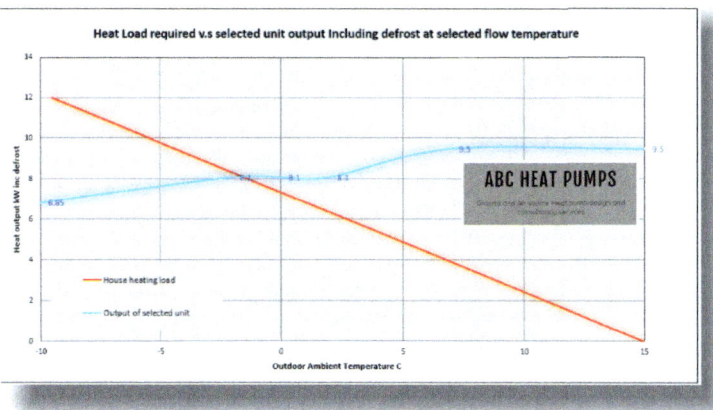

Looking at the graph above, In Manchester we would design at -3C (see q 19) but I have extended the graph to -10C, note that we need no heating if its +15C outside, 8kW at -2C outside and 12kW at -10C.

The graph is drawn from the data given by the manufacturers in a technical data book, it's called a capacity table:

This is for a Midea 10kW model. A few things to note, firstly the Midea CANNOT supply water at +65C is its colder than 5 degrees C outside.

Look at the 55 degree C column, it can give 7097 Watts at 0 degrees C ambient but only 2615 Watts at -20C.

What output will it give at -2C? you have to use a calculator to work it out.

LWT		45			50			55			60			65		
Outdoor air temperature[°C]	CL	CAP	COP	PI	CAP	COP	PI	CAP	COP	PI	CAP	COP	PI	CAP	COP	PI
-25	max	2815	1.30	2170	/	/	/	/	/	/	/	/	/	/	/	/
	norm	2638	1.29	2050	/	/	/	/	/	/	/	/	/	/	/	/
	min	1773	1.29	1371	/	/	/	/	/	/	/	/	/	/	/	/
-20	max	3697	1.61	2291	3175	1.41	2258	2615	1.25	2097	/	/	/	/	/	/
	norm	3427	1.62	2109	2956	1.42	2078	2516	1.25	2005	/	/	/	/	/	/
	min	2292	1.64	1397	2191	1.44	1525	1909	1.27	1506	/	/	/	/	/	/
-15	max	5288	2.00	2649	4669	1.73	2705	4937	1.69	2916	3994	1.41	2841	/	/	/
	norm	4690	2.03	2311	4160	1.76	2358	4552	1.72	2647	3718	1.41	2642	/	/	/
	min	3384	2.06	1643	3222	1.79	1800	3357	1.75	1924	2836	1.43	1985	/	/	/
-10	max	6770	2.47	2741	6317	2.20	2878	6066	1.99	3049	5187	1.81	2861	/	/	/
	norm	6141	2.50	2457	5755	2.23	2578	5533	2.01	2751	4777	1.81	2646	/	/	/
	min	4103	2.55	1610	4289	2.28	1884	4198	2.05	2047	3724	1.84	2022	/	/	/
-7	max	6944	2.52	2756	6479	2.24	2892	6222	2.03	3065	5320	1.85	2876	/	/	/
	norm	5986	2.62	2288	5481	2.31	2373	5301	2.09	2533	4687	1.89	2486	/	/	/
	min	3410	2.67	1279	3382	2.35	1437	3571	2.13	1674	3415	1.92	1777	/	/	/
-5	max	7444	2.69	2772	7345	2.46	2986	6447	2.19	2944	6040	2.02	2997	/	/	/
	norm	6491	2.79	2329	6287	2.54	2479	5557	2.26	2461	5381	2.05	2621	/	/	/
	min	3595	2.84	1266	3775	2.59	1460	3649	2.30	1585	3708	2.09	1771	/	/	/
0	max	8090	2.94	2752	8111	2.75	2955	7097	2.38	2988	6849	2.17	3156	/	/	/
	norm	7160	3.05	2351	7389	2.79	2644	6330	2.41	2631	6034	2.17	2783	/	/	/
	min	3568	3.12	1144	4120	2.86	1439	3804	2.47	1543	4061	2.22	1828	/	/	/
5	max	8694	3.38	2569	8304	3.00	2764	7562	2.76	2740	7110	2.46	2885	3887	1.19	3266
	norm	7624	3.54	2154	7499	3.09	2428	6684	2.82	2367	6207	2.49	2496	3316	1.22	2721
	min	4095	3.64	1125	4468	3.18	1405	4280	2.91	1473	4430	2.56	1730	2468	1.24	1994

Midea M thermal Mono Engineering Data Book
kW-Maximum heating CAP

The output of the heat pump falls as it gets colder, but the amount of heat we need goes up.

The skill of the designer is to size the heat pump to be just big enough to do the job. If we had a prolonged period of cold weather at -10C the unit would no longer be big enough. The unit would not stop operating but it could no longer maintain 21C in every room.

At -10 in this case the heat pump only gives just over half the heat required. The room temperature would drop quite dramatically in this case. But it's never -10C for more than a few hours and the house will have heat stored in the bricks and mortar, it will take time to drop in temperature. Remember in Manchester the temperature falls below -3C degrees for 72 hours every year.

21 Will I run out of hot water?

When we work out what hot water cylinder you need, we allow 55 litres of hot water per person, per day.

A normal shower uses 10 litres a minute

A bath holds about 100L of water.

When we design your heating system, we typically aim for the heat pump to be able to recover the hot water cylinder from cold to hot in 60-90 minutes.

When we are carrying out the survey, we will discuss with the homeowner what your hot usage is now and try to match it with the new system.

Example: if you have a tiny cylinder now and never run out of water this is easy to achieve. If you have a huge hot water cylinder and are always running out of water, we will put a much larger tank in.

It's your house, you can have as much or as little hot water as you like, we will incorporate this into our design and spec.

22 What is the carbon saving from a heat pump and what is a carbon footprint?

Everyone knows there is a thing called a carbon footprint, its how much Carbon you are responsible for, everyone knows it needs to be smaller. But Literally no one I speak too knows what their carbon footprint is. We need to sort out a message that is easy to visualise and understand.

Most people say they want to reduce climate change, but they don't know how, they would also like it to happen without impacting on their lives.

As an average citizen of the UK, I'm responsible for 9000 kgs of CO_2 per year, put more simply 1 kg of CO_2 <u>every hour</u> ends up in the air because of me. That is a lot of pollution.

3 cans of coke weigh 1kg. That's convenient and easy to

imagine.

- One can represents the weight of CO_2 I chuff into the air at home with my heating and energy use.

- Another can represent the weight of CO2 I chuff into the air because I travel around.
- And the last can represents the weight of CO2 from all the stuff I buy and use.

We need to get this level of pollution down and fast, tomorrow would be a good day to start. I think it would be cool if everything we bought had the number of kgs of CO2 needed to make it was printed on the side, just like nutritional info is now. Then at least you could see how you were doing in reducing your CO2.

So how do we do it? let's make the easy steps first.

- Either move a lot less or move more efficiently, that means go for a more efficient or an electric car.
- Heat your house with a heat pump, they are available now, you don't have to wait for a silver bullet, the boiler has to go. And while you are at it turn off some of the lights.
- Buy less stuff, or at least buy stuff with a smaller CO2 footprint and throw less away and maybe even try some recycling or repurposing.

But it might be time for us all to think about whether we are going to do something about our level of CO2 pollution or just accept that CO2 levels are going to rise and we just have to deal with it.

A heat pump is a **renewable heating technology see q 23** which does not burn fossil fuels at source. Switching to a heat pump can easily save 1000 kgs or 1 tonne of Co2 per person per year in your house. A heat pump turns you from a 9000 kgs of Co2 to an 8000kgs of Co2 person, just for changing a boiler. Simple huh.

When your MCS design is completed, the design gives a more

accurate carbon saving figure for you and your house.

Of course, the electricity they use may be made by burning fossil fuels but the % of our electricity from renewable sources is constantly increasing so they become more and more

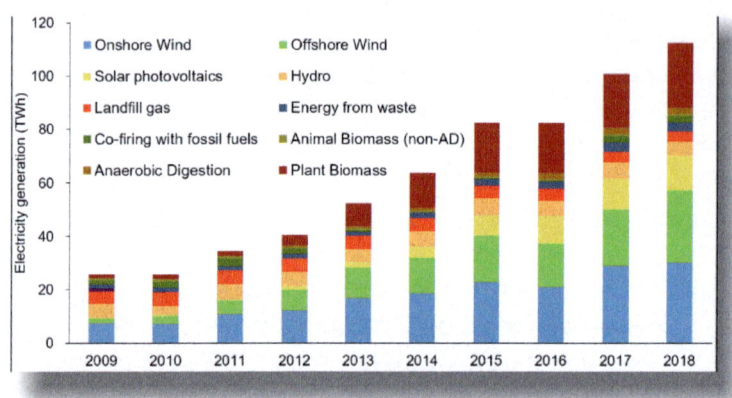

renewable on a day-by-day basis. See Graph.

Renewables are popular because they reduce the amount of CO2 you emit each year which in turn helps to reduce **global warming**. Currently the UK imports approximately 50% of its energy, by switching from a boiler to a heat pump you are increasing the UK's and your own, security of energy supply.

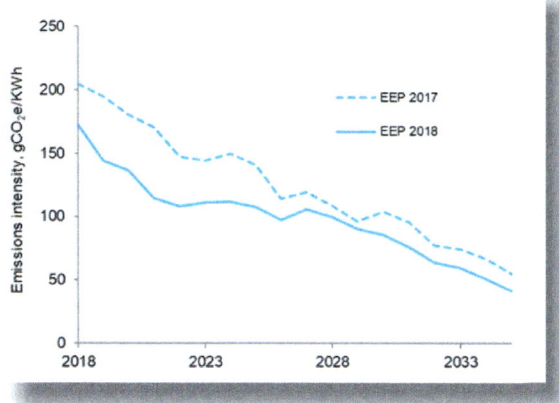

In 2018 (on average) every kWhr of electricity supplied to your home came with 175 grams of CO2 emissions. But this is predicted to decline as more and more renewables provide our electricity.

So as electricity gets greener by 2030 your 1 tonne or 1000kgs a year saving will become 2 tonnes as the electricity grid gets less carbon intensive.

23 If they run on electricity, how can they be renewable?

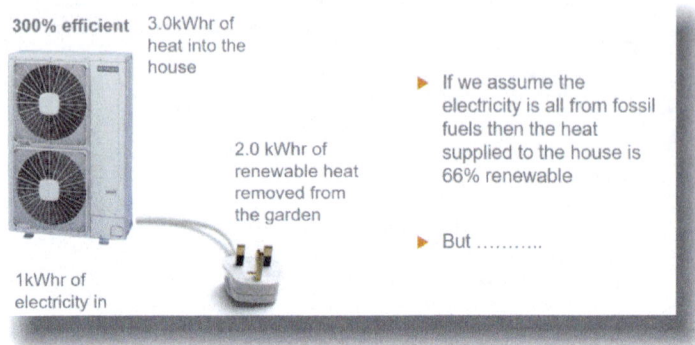

On 7th January 2022 at Midday this was how we made our electricity in the UK

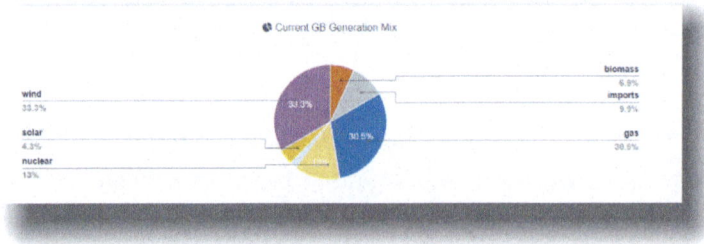

https://www.carbonintensity.org.uk/ 7/1/22

40.4% is from fossil fuels, the rest is renewable.

Heat pumps use 1kWhr of electricity to gather 2 kWhrs of heat from the garden and put 3 kWhrs of heat into the house.

To produce the 3kWhrs of heat we use :
0.4 kW hrs of electricity is from fossil fuels and 0.6 kWhrs is from renewables. 0.4/3 = 13% of the heat is not from renewable sources, 87% is renewable.

24 I have a solar thermal tank already can I use it with my heat pump?

Solar thermal works by the sun warming special tubes containing water up on the roof. The tubes are designed to capture as much heat as possible from the sun and use it to warm up the water in the pipes.

Here is a cut away of a solar thermal tube. It's basically a solar boiler.

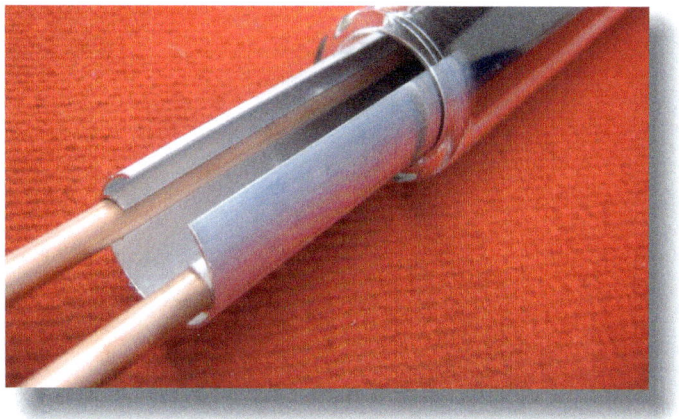

This warm water is pumped from the roof through a dedicated coil in your hot water cylinder heating the water you bathe in.

The only difference between a normal heat pump hot water cylinder and a heat pump solar cylinder is the number of coils inside. The solar cylinder has one coil for the heat pump and one for the solar thermal, a normal heat pump cylinder only has one coil.

The heat pump uses a second completely separate coil to heat the water on cloudy days and at night.

To be really successful it's nice to set the heat pump to only heat the tank in winter and at night and let the solar cover the warmer months.

25 Can I have a Solar PV diverter, Eddi, Solar I-boost and a heat pump?

We are often asked if the solar PV on the roof can directly power the heat pump. The answer is not really.

But you can buy a device from My Energi called Eddi or an I boost which monitors the output of your solar PV panels, If there is spare electricity being produced it will power up the immersion heater in the hot water cylinder providing free hot water.

The genius of these solar diverters is you don't need to be producing 3kW of electricity to power the 3kW immersion, using clever control by basically switching the power on and off hundreds of times a second the diverter can supply as little as a few hundred Watts to the immersion trickling heat into the cylinder as the PV panels produce it. It's better to do this than send the spare electricity back to the grid.

Think of it as a solar thermal hot water system but without the inconvenience of any pipes from the roof, through the loft to the hot water cylinder.

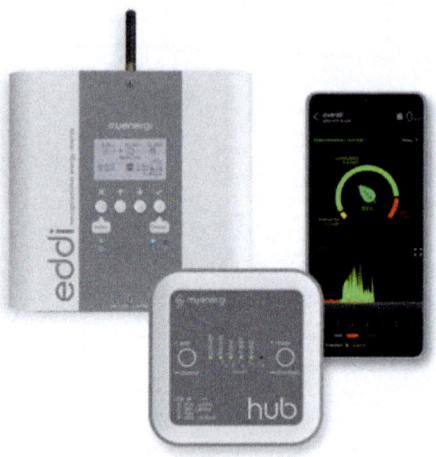

It is NOT possible to reliably run the heat pump directly off the PV panels.
The solar diverter cannot control the heat pump accurately enough to do this. Its similar to trying to run your lights off the diverter, if its switching on and off rapidly the lights would be very dim and would annoy you, the heat pump is the same it needs a nice steady power supply.

It's common for people to assume that if they can make electricity on the roof with the PV system, they could use this to power the heat pump to heat the house, but Solar powered heating is a myth, the problem is the heating tends to need to run in Winter at night not in Summer when the sun is shining.

In this graph I plotted the average monthly output of a 4kW PV system against the average monthly consumption of an 8kW heat pump system.

Note how from March to October the PV can provide all the hot water from the solar panels assumes 300L cylinder and 4kW PV system.

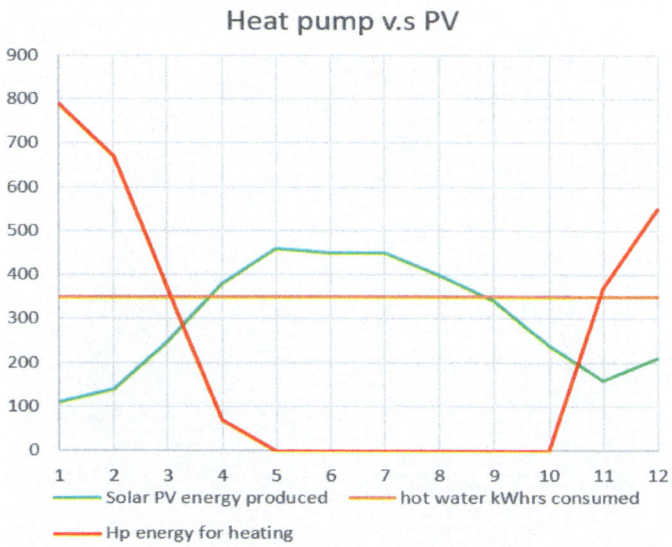

Using a solar diverter, we estimate that the heating and hot water run cost can be reduced by 8% compared to a system with no PV on the roof.

26 Will a battery power my heat pump?

There are many types of domestic batteries available, the Tesla power wall is a typical and popular example, in 2022 a power

wall can hold 13.5kW hrs of electricity.

Put into context that means a power wall could run a kettle, an 8kW heat pump (running flat out) or an immersion heater for 4 ½ hours continuously.

If we take an 8kW heat pump, we can show how many units of electricity it will use on an average day. It is obviously higher in the winter and lower in the summer.

If we assume the battery is full every day, either from the electricity made from the Photo Voltaic panels in the house or from cheap rate electricity from the grid, we can show what percentage of the heating we could cover with one batteries worth of storage.

In this example below we could power an 8kW heat pump 7 months of the year, the other 5 months we would still need help from the grid.

	hp energy per day	% covered by battery
January	37	37%
February	33	41%
March	23	58%
April	14	100%
May	8	174%
June	4	348%
July	2	697%
August	2	697%
September	8	174%
October	12	116%
November	23	58%
December	29	46%

It's obvious that a battery storage system can be very cost effective with a heat pump.

Some of the better solar and battery companies can run very realistic simulations of your house with these systems connected. You can assume a 20-25% saving can be made with this sort of system compared to a heat pump with no PV and no battery.

27 Can I combine my heat pump with a wood burner?

Many homes have a wood burner, in most cases it is free standing and not connected to the wet heating system at all. However, some have a coil inside which can be used to heat hot water, a bit like a boiler and use this to heat other rooms in the house.

There are several restrictions to doing this because the wood burner is not a controllable heat source, it's possible that the water in the boiler could boil if it's in there too long. There are regulations about how this is done. It's not something most heating engineers have the qualification to do so, I would recommend avoiding it where possible.

If the homeowner insists however, it is possible to connect a wood burner into the heating part of the heat pump circuit, we normally recommend it is done using a buffer vessel with a coil.

We set up the system so that if the wood burner warms the water over 50 degrees C the heat pump stops operating. It's important that the heat pump does not have very hot water returning to it. If this happens you can get overheating alarms.

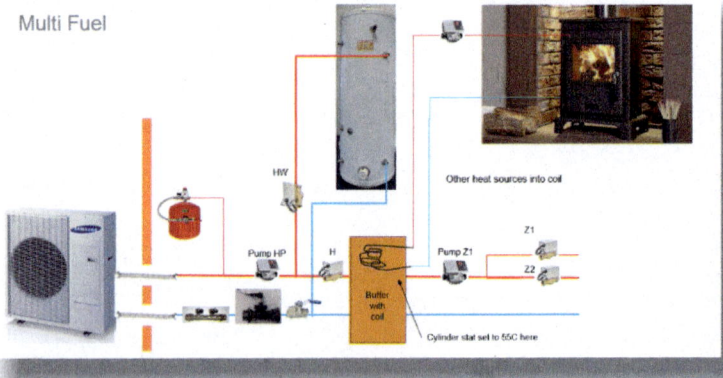

28 Can I combine my heat pump with a boiler? Hybrids explained

In older poorly insulated and very large buildings we meet 2 problems, the first being the heat load is very high so we can't cover it with a single heat pump and the second being the homeowner does not want to replace the radiators or hot water cylinder.

Installing more than one heat pump is not a problem and is a really good solution, but if you have more than one heat pump installed you always have to apply for planning permission, this can often kill the deal.

There are two separate solutions for these problems:

If the house is too big for a single heat pump, using a backup heat source. System design temperature between 40 and 55C.

In this case we could use a heat pump and another heat source, either a backup boiler or an inline electric heater. In mild conditions the heat pump will be able to cover all of your heating an hot water needs, when the weather turns colder the heat pump will reach its maximum output and will need help. At this point it will ask its backup heater or boiler to assist. Both the heat pump and the backup boiler will operate at the same time.

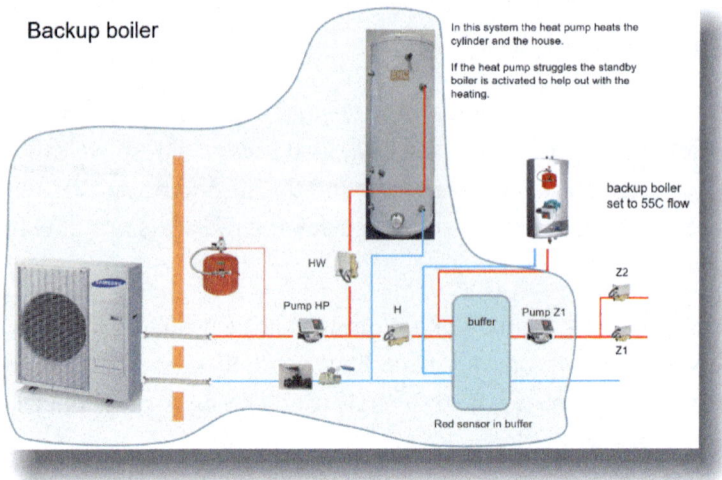

IT is essential that the boiler / backup and the heat pump operate at exactly the same temperature. If the boiler runs at a higher temperature the heat pump will be flooded with warm return water and it will assume the house needs less heat, it will turn off the boiler and try to do all the work itself. The boiler will cycle in and out like the fiddler's elbow. This is not a good solution.

Backup systems only work if the radiators or underfloor are designed to operate at the heat pumps outlet temperate ere, typically between 40 and 55C.

If the homeowner wants to keep the old radiators, a Hybrid system. System design temperature greater than 55C.

In our industry we like to over-complicate everything with stupid names, I call these systems dual fuel or hybrids. Some people call them Bi-valent, it's a ridiculous name but some people think calling them this makes them sound clever, it doesn't.

A hybrid is a system which uses both a fossil fuel boiler and a heat pump. It's exactly like a hybrid car, when you want to go slowly you use the electric system and when you want to go fast you use the engine.

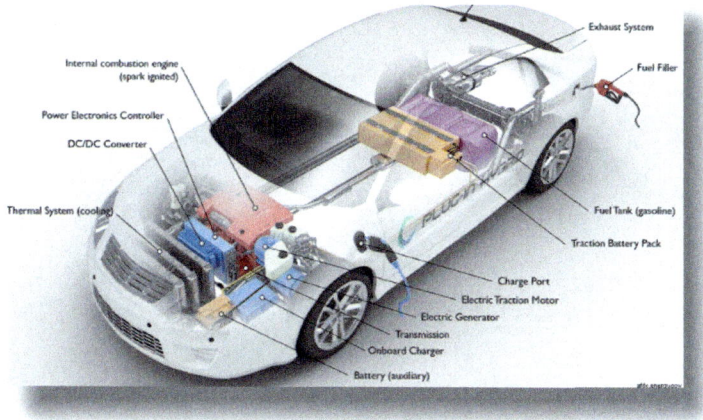

The idea is the homeowner can embrace the renewable heating technology but still have the fossil fuel boiler to fall back on. Some consumers prefer this to an all-out heat pump only solution. Hybrid systems were very popular a few years ago when people were worried about whether a heat pump would work, people liked the idea of having the trusty old boiler as a backup.

Nowadays with ultra-high temperature heat pumps operating with outputs of 16kW at -10C ambient and run temperatures of up to 80 degrees C, (see q10) hybrids and backup units are much less often used.

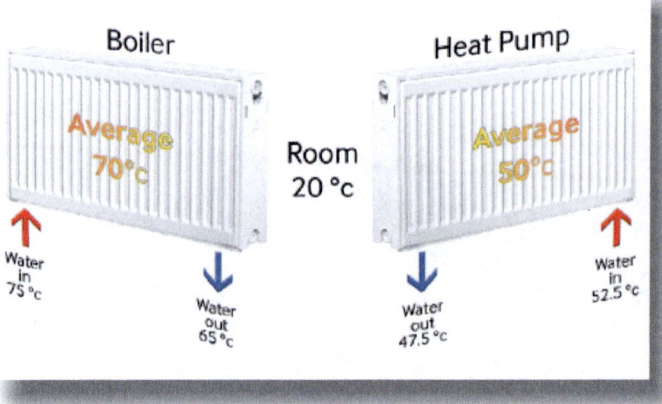

In a hybrid heat pump, we use the heat pump to heat the radiators to 50 degrees C, this is ok in milder weather but typically when the temperature outside falls below 3 degrees C we need the radiators to be warmer to keep the house up to temperature. In a hybrid we switch the heat pump off at 3 degrees C ambient (outdoor) temperature and start the boiler up. The boiler will run at 70 degrees C raising the output of the radiators just when you need it. In a hybrid system the boiler and heat pump NEVER heat the house at the same time. They are two different temperature systems.

In most hybrid systems the heat pump only heats the house it cannot heat the hot water.

In April 2022 the new government grant will NOT cover hybrid heat pump systems at all. If you have a hybrid the grant will be £0. From 2013-2022 we used to put a heat meter into the heat pump circuit to measure how much of the work the heat pump did. The RHI grant would pay out on the reading from the heat meter.

The two main types of Hybrid:

Combi hybrid, where the house has a combi boiler and no hot water cylinder.

The combi hybrid is a nice simple solution, we add a heat pump, 2 pumps and a plate heat exchanger all highlit in the diagram below to your existing heating system, the boiler and the rads are all left in exactly the same place they are in now.

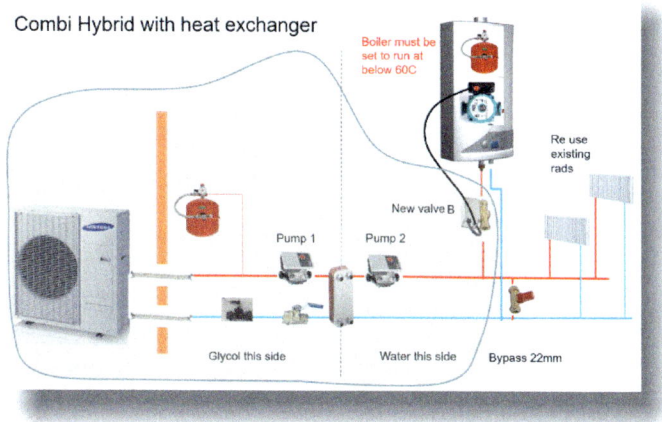

In this system the combi boiler will only help the heat pump heat the house, the combi will provide all your hot water just like it always did in the past. This mans you don't need a new hot water cylinder. The old radiators and pipework are all left in place we don't need to change them.

System hybrid, where the house has a boiler and existing hot water cylinder.

The system hybrid is a simple solution, we add a heat pump, 2 pumps and a plate heat exchanger all highlit in the diagram below to your existing heating system, the boiler, hot water cylinder and the rads are all left in exactly the same place they are in now.

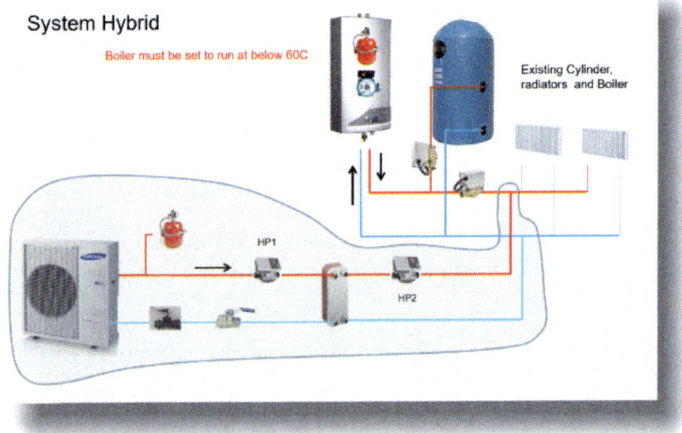

In this system the boiler will only help the heat pump heat the house, the boiler will provide all your hot water in the existing hot water cylinder just like it always did in the past. This mans you don't need a new hot water cylinder. The old radiators and pipework are all left in place we don't need to change them.

It is very difficult to get the heat pump to also heat the hot water so it is generally the norm to connect it up as per the above.

29 Can I cool with a heat pump?

Air source heat pumps are clever, not only can they heat your house, but they can also cool. In any refrigeration system reversing from cooling to heating is simple. We use a thing called a 4-way valve. Simply by moving a valve we can make the hot bit cold and the cold bit hot, it's a simple trick of reversing the direction the refrigerant goes round the system.

If you have a heat pump installed, it will heat the hot water tank and supply all the heat for your radiators and underfloor heating. Essentially all its doing is cooling the garden down, by sucking the heat out of the air and dumping that heat into the water going round your house. If you reversed the refrigerant direction (easy when you know how) you could cool the water in the house and dump the heat in the garden. That means you have a machine that could cool your house and it is free, its already installed.

But sorry to be a spoil sport, there are 3 reasons why you could do it but you would be an fool if you did.

No 1 you are going to get wet

If you pump cold water around your system every single bit of it that's made of metal will sweat, think of a cold can of beer on a warm day, it sweats because the water in the air condenses on cold surfaces. You are going to have wet pipes and dripping radiators. You could lag the pipes and put rags under the rads. Underfloor heating is worse, you could get to a position where you had condensation on the floor.

No 2 cold air does not rise.

So, you've got rags under the rads and the cooling on, the cold air pours off the radiators and sinks to the floor, cold air sinks. So, if it's hot you have to lie on the floor to keep cold. It's beginning to look like a really bad idea but just when you thought it couldn't get worse here goes:

No 3 the cooling won't be powerful enough.

Your heating is designed to supply heat in the coldest weather, when we do a heat loss, we assume it's cold and dark outside and you want the rooms at 21 degrees C. We don't take into consideration all the people, dogs, cats, ovens, kettles, TVs etc which you could have in the house, these all help by adding heat, so we see them as a bonus. But if you do a heat gain calculation for cooling you have to fight all the heat coming into the room from the sun, the dogs, cats, people, TVs etc.

As an example, a standard house built in 2000 would need about 40 Watts of heat for every metre square of floor area, but in cooling it would need over 100 Watts per metre square. The cooling load is more than twice the heating load.

Your system has a design flow temperature typically 50C for rads, that's 30 degrees higher than the room temperature and 45C for underfloor heating, or 25 degrees above the room temperature.

The heating / cooling load is proportional to the difference between the water in the rads and the room temperature. Hot rads emit more heat than cold ones. It's the same in cooling, cold rad = good cooling, tepid rad = poor cooling.

If you want to double the capacity out of the radiators or UFH you have to double the temperature difference between the room and the water in the rads/ under floor heating. So that means running the water through radiators are 21 - (30*2) = minus 40 degrees C. You will be making ice on the radiators if you did this and the water in the system would be like slush puppy even with glycol. I implore you do not try this at home, you won't be covered by warranty.

When you are offered cooling using a heat pump, it is possible but it's not going to be real cooling like you get with the air con in your car, it's just going to take a tiny bit of heat away. On some heat pumps we can offer a dew point sensor which means the radiators and UFH never sweat, to do this we can only drop the water a few degrees below the room temperature. The result is you only get a tiny cooling effect which you will only feel on your ankles. It's not very good but it's cheap to do.

But it's not all bad news, if you want cooling using your air source heat pumps. We can put a separate, insulated cooling system onto a heat pump like this below. The cooling zone would use fan coils designed for cooling and normal rads in heating.

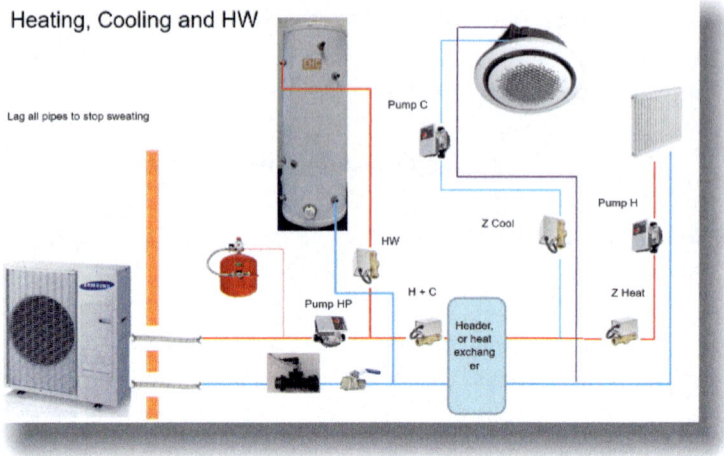

Or you could do it properly, if you want cooling buy air conditioning, put it next to your heat pump. One does heat one does cool.

The unit on the right is an air source heat pump, it gets a grant of £5000. It needed 78 pages of forms filling in to get the grant, the homeowner needed to tell the DNO (electricity board) it was going in and get the electricity supply approved.

The unit on the left is an air-conditioning unit, (air to air Heat pump) it doesn't use water at all, the installer just installed it, no grant, no paperwork, no DNO, no planning permission and it cost under half of the one on the right. Oh, and it heats too.

30 Am I better waiting for Hydrogen boiler or nuclear fusion?

Although Hydrogen will have its place to play in the energy mix in the future it's very hard to determine when.

The same goes for Nuclear Fusion

Both are great solutions but are not currently available to buy.

When they will be ready is impossible to predict.

31 Why isn't there a combi heat pump?

Discuss: if you have an electric shower what happens to the water temperature if you turn up the water speed?

How many kWs is your electric shower?

How quickly can your electric shower go from 0- full power?

How long does a heat pump take to go from 0-100% power?

Heat pumps are not fast acting machines, typically if you send a run signal to the unit it thinks about starting up for about 3 minutes as it does its pre-start-up checks. It then enters a start-up phase and gently ramps up to full speed. This process can and usually does take between 5 and 10 minutes.

Now imagine you were in the shower; you turn on the tap and wait 10 minutes for the heat pump to get up to speed and make the water warm.

It's impossible to make a heat pump heat instantly, so we store the hot water in a hot water cylinder so you can access it whenever you like, the cylinder means you are not at the mercy of the heat pumps start up procedure.

The next problem is capacity or oomph. A combi boiler gives 24kW of heat, this means it can heat 12 litres of water from cold water temperature 10 degrees C to 45 degrees C every minute. That's plenty for a very hot shower.

An 8kW heat pump would only manage to heat 4 litres of water a minute, you would struggle to get wet with 4 litres a minute. If a comb heat pump was ever invented, you would have to get a massive unit to provide the hot water.

32 Can you use more than one heat pump if the house is big?

Yes, you can have as many heat pumps as you like.

But there are two problems:

The first is you always need planning permission for more than

1 heat pump

And second, does the house have a large enough power supply?

The average UK house has a 100 Amp power supply, you need 32 Amps for the cooker and hob, 13 Amps for the kettle and a few other items. This leaves 50 Amps spare. A single 16kW heat pump needs a 32 Amp power supply.

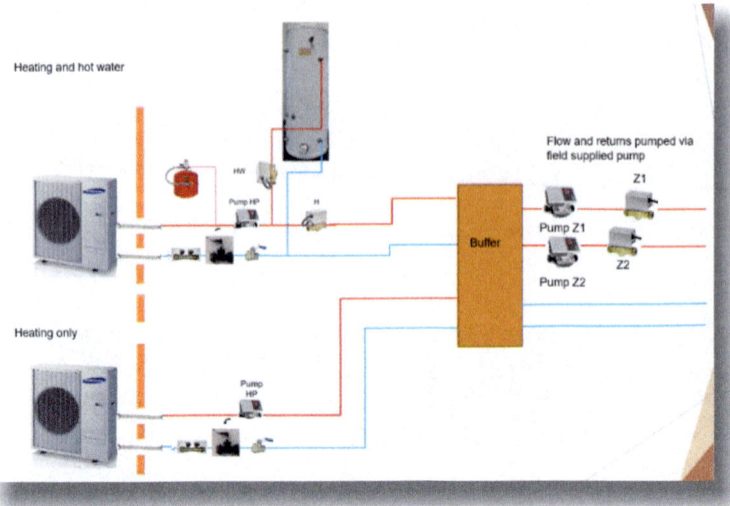

Multiple units are tubed up like this. We combine them into a single heating system so both units help heat the whole house.

There are a number of advantages with this configuration. If only a small amount of the house needs heating only one heat pump will operate. One heat pump can concentrate on hot water while the other continues to heat the house. If the house needs lots of heat both units heat the house. If one unit breaks down the other will continue to heat the house on its own while you wait for the engineer.

When we design the system, we use a buffer vessel to connect the two units together. It's important to get the pipe sizes correct. Each 28mm pipe can only carry 16.8kW of heat so it's impossible to have 2 heat pumps coming into the buffer but only one 28mm pipe leaving to serve the heating system.

33 What is the biggest heat pump you can buy?

Most domestic heat pumps are only 16kW of output. The reason they are this size is this is the biggest the unit can be when connecting it to a domestic power supply. We like to limit the power supply to 32 Amps, it's the same size supply you

would use for an electric shower or electric cooker Hob.

In commercial applications they have access to much larger power supplies. The biggest air source heat pumps are over 1MW or 1000kWs. They tend to be designed mostly for cooling, so they call them chillers but some of them also heat. this one was 1200kWs the pipework is 300mm in diameter.

34 If heat pumps are expensive, can I get a grant?

Yes, there have been grants for heat pumps for the last 8 years. In 2014 a grant called the **renewable heat incentive** was introduced. It was in place until April 2022. The RHI paid every quarter for 7 years. It was capped at about £1500 a year or a total of £11000 for an air source heat pump. Smaller and well insulated houses got smaller grants.

In April 2022 the **boiler upgrade Scheme,** BUS was introduced. This replaced the RHI with a single £5000 payment as the heat pump was installed, the BUS scheme is a flat payment no matter the size of your heat pump or house. As a result, its more beneficial in smaller installations.

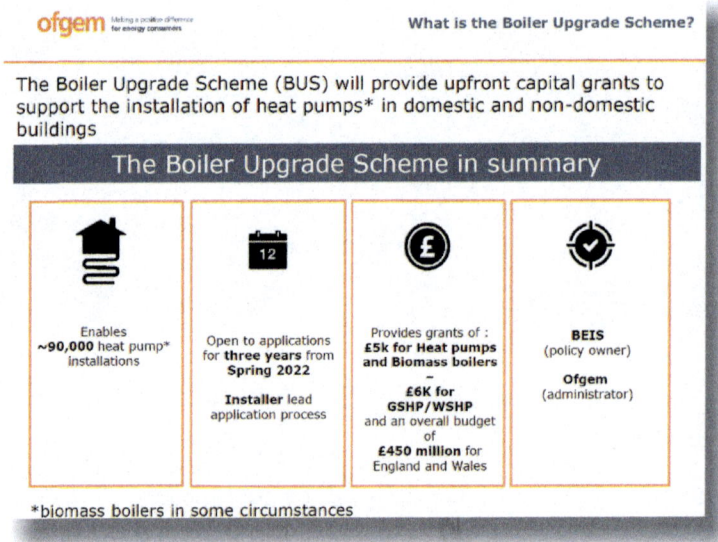

Under the boiler upgrade scheme there are some simple rules to follow:

1. You have to have an energy performance certificate EPC for the house, you can find it here https://www.gov.uk/find-

energy-certificate If you can't find your EPC, you have to have a new one, they cost about £50. Mr google will help you find a local EPC assessor. See q 37

2 The government are keen to only support you if you have done some insulation work to your house, paying people to heat houses which are thermal disasters would not be a good idea so, If your house does not have cavity wall insulation AND loft insulation 200mm thick the EPC will highlight this. 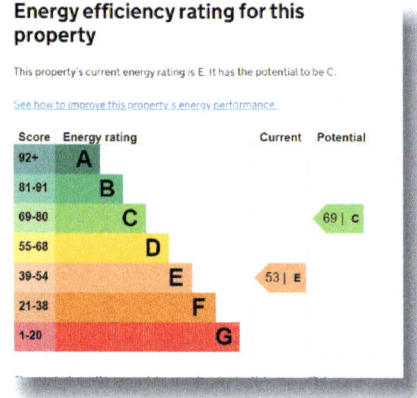 There will be no grant until these two simple jobs are not complete and the new EPC shows its done. If you don't have cavities or a loft you do not have to have this work done. See q41 for exceptions.

3. The Boiler upgrade scheme covers any house and some commercial buildings where the boiler is being removed and replaced with a heat pump. You cannot keep the boiler in place.

4. The installer must be MCS accredited as must the heat pump. MCS is a quality standard, installers must go through a process to get this accreditation, it is not a simple job and can be costly. If your installer is not MCS accredited, or you buy a non MCS heat pump there will be no grant.

5. The installer will handle the whole grant application process for you, they get the grant payment, not you, they will quote you for the work and will inform Ofgem who administer the BUS vouchers that they are doing this, once you accept the quote you will have to pay the balance of the quote, the installer will

get their £5k from the government a few days after you have signed you are happy.

6. The boiler upgrade scheme covers all boilers which burn fossil fuels, gas, LPG and Oil, it also covers electric storage heaters and electric boilers. It does not cover replacing an old heat pump with a new one.

35 How do I get the BUS Boiler upgrade Scheme voucher / grant?

The first step to getting the boiler upgrade Scheme grant is to speak to an MCS heat pump installer. Mr google will help here.

Your MCS installer will have a BUS account with Ofgem so they can receive the vouchers.

Then it will follow this process:

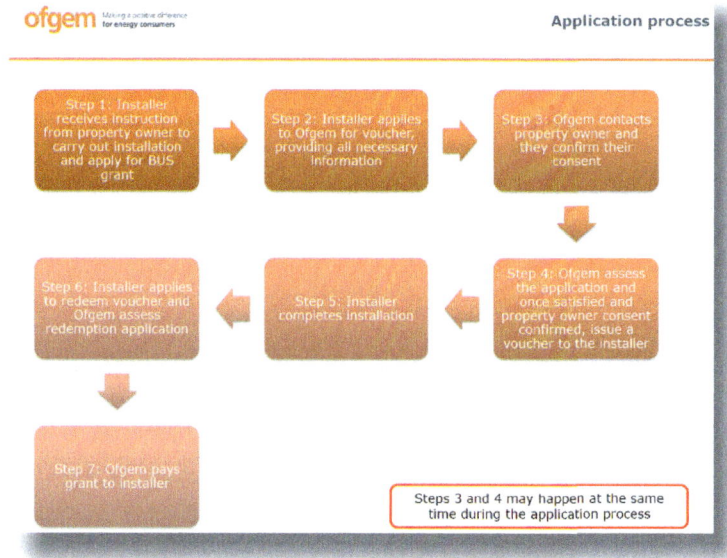

You cannot get the grant as a homeowner, its paid to the installer, they will pass the saving onto you.

36 What is an Energy Performance Certificate, EPC?

An EPC is an energy performance certificate, you can check if your house has one here https://www.gov.uk/find-energy-certificate

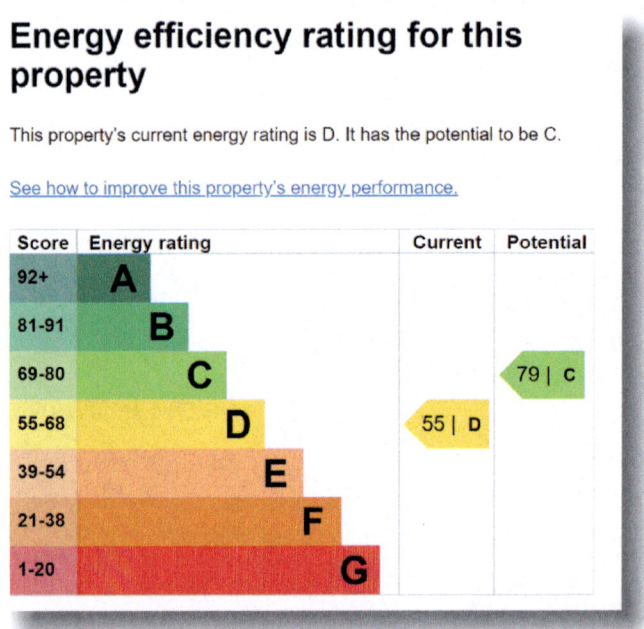

To get an EPC you must find a local assessor, there are hundreds of them across the country, they will come and survey the house. Mr Google can help you find one locally.

The EPC assessor is looking for insulation in the walls, floors ceilings etc. They use a piece of software which they enter the details in to establish how much energy your house will use per year and where improvements could be made and the likely impact of doing these modifications.

The EPC survey **is not the same** as the survey for the heat load calculation we use to work out what heat pump you require, they are looking at slightly different information. The EPC works out the average energy used over the year and points to improvements you could make. The heat load calculation works out what the maximum amount of heat you will need on the coldest day of the year and takes into consideration what the

Heating use in this property

Heating a property usually makes up the majority of energy costs.

Estimated energy used to heat this property

Space heating	17437 kWh per year
Water heating	2765 kWh per year

Potential energy savings by installing insulation

Type of insulation	Amount of energy saved
Loft insulation	4779 kWh per year

house is made of today.

37 How do I know what heat pump I need at home?

There are many ways to choose a heat pump, varying from a guess to an educated guess and finally selecting the unit properly using a full room by room heat load calculation.

In the bad old days before there were any grants see Q35 people would guess the size of unit needed, often with some poor results and very unhappy consumers. Like this frozen-up unit, this is what happens if the unit is woefully under sized for the house.

It's perfectly acceptable to use some quick calculations to obtain budget figures for a heat pump, but to get the BUS boiler upgrade Scheme voucher a full heat load survey must be completed. There are no short cuts.

An educated guess is where we would use data from a house we have worked on before, there are many apps for this, I prefer a simple grid like this.

heat load calcuator Grid

year / floor area	100m^2	150m^2	200m^2	250m^2	300m^2	400m^2	500m^2
pre 1918	12000	16500	20000	25000	30000	40000	50000
1918-1970	10000	13500	16000	20000	24000	32000	40000
1970-1990	9300	12000	14200	17750	21300	28400	35500
1990-2000	8400	11250	13000	16250	19500	26000	32500
2000-2010	6000	7500	8800	11000	13200	17600	22000
2010-2016	4600	6000	7200	9000	10800	14400	18000
2016-2020	3600	5250	6600	8250	9900	13200	16500
2016-2020 with HRV	2900	4200	5400	6750	8100	10800	13500

These are very good ways of getting close to the unit you need and supplying budget figures but there really is only one way to size a heat pump, properly. The proper way to do it is a heat load calculation.

A surveyor will come to the house, measure every room, ceiling height, window, radiator and check all the insulation in the loft and the walls and floor. This info will be input into a tool which will tell the surveyor exactly what size heat pump you will need in the house and what radiators will need to be changed.

Good heat load calculators will also estimate accurately what the run costs will be, what they are now and work out your carbon savings.

The installers will give you the results of the heat load calculation usually after you have committed to buy. In an average 3 bed house the survey, the calculations and system selection can take a full day's work. Surveyors will not want you the homeowner to run off with the design to get other quotes without paying for this service.

38 Are old houses ok with heat pumps / how old? Isn't new build better?

Discuss:

In a new house you can design the heating to suit any system, everything is new.

In an old house the homeowner will want you to try to use as much of the equipment on site as possible.

What parts of the system can you think they would want to reuse?

Heat pumps are just machines we use to replace boilers. No one would ask "can I put a boiler in a big house, or an old house". The bigger the house the bigger the boiler, it's no different with

a heat pump.

The first problem we have to overcome, when we propose a heat pump is old houses will very likely already have a heating system the homeowner doesn't really want changed too much.

If there is an ancient heating system with old pipework and radiators its often a good idea to upgrade this whenever you do any work to the heating system, whether you install a boiler or a heat pump. But people think that this work only needs doing with heat pumps, usually because they haven't had experience with any heating upgrades over the last years. Boilers last 15 years.

When did you last have any work done on your heating system at home?

The second problem to overcome is old houses have poor insulation which mean they have a bigger heat loss.

Example. A brand new 3 bed, 125m^2 house will only need a 6kW heat pump, the same house but 100 years old will need a 16kW heat pump. It's because old houses leak heat badly and new ones do not.

So, if your house is a combination of old and large there comes a point where we need to install more than one heat pump. Generally speaking domestic heat pumps only go up to 16kW output. Putting more than one heat pump in is easy and very common, but the costs rise quickly, and multiple units can be difficult to hide in the garden.

In new houses we can design the whole heating system before the house is built, so everything goes seamlessly together, it's easier. Also, the house would have to be massive (over 450m^2) before you need to install more than one heat pump. New houses are just easier for any heating system.

Many heat pump installers just work in the new building sector because it's easier to get everything right if everything is new and installed by just one team.

39 Do I have to modify my house to be heat pump ready? do I have to insulate it?

Insulation can make a very dramatic difference to the heat load

or the amount of heating your house requires.

This is a picture of an average UK house, when it was built in the 1930s it had no loft insulation, no cavity wall insulation, single glazed wooden windows, and a vented wooden floor. (You can see air bricks close to the ground to let the air in) It was originally heated using open fireplaces burning coal.

If we do a heat loss on this property as it was built in 1930 it would look like this.

MCS Heat loss In accordance with EN12831

ABC HEAT PUMPS
Ground and air source Heat pump design and consultancy services

Results

Total Heat loss	17761	W
Heated floor area	128.0	m^2
Average W/m²	139	m^2

the design temperatures are set in MCS, this design temperature is altered 0.6C for every 100m above sea level.

Location

location	London
MCS Ambient temp	-1.8
MCS Ground temp	10.2
height above sea level	30.0
Corrected Amb temp	-2.0
Corrected Gnd temp	10.0

Building Details

		U-value	% of total heat
External Wall type	1918 - 1970 cavity wall no insulation	1.60	29%
Window type	pre 1990 single glazed wood	4.80	16%
Roof / Ceiling type	pre 1980 no insulation	1.50	27%
Floor type	pre 1918 wood floor vented	1.75	8%
Ventilation loss	Living rooms/Hallways	1.50	20%

Note at the top how the heat loss is 17761 Watts or 17.6kW, that is the equivalent of 6 electric blower fires. If we divide this by the floor area that's 139 Watts needed for every square metre of floor, upstairs and downstairs. That is huge. (A 2020 built house would be 25 Watts for every square metre of floor).

At 18kW heat load you would need 2 heat pumps to heat this house. No one makes a domestic heat pump big enough to fight the heat load.

We can look at where the heat is going, Note how:

5kW loss is through the walls, 2.8kW through the windows, 4.8kW through the loft, 1.4kW through the floor and 3.5kW though drafts.

Current Heating System	correct on 5/11/21
	estimated run cost /yr
Natural gas OFGEM	£ 3,206.74
Energy Cost	p/kWhr or litre
Cost of Gas pence per kWhr	6.5
Cost of electricity pence per kWhr	20.3
Cost of oil pence per Litre	58.0
Cost of LPG, pence per litre	68.0

New system estimated run cost per Year	
	£ 2,448.99

Left as it is this house is a thermal disaster, it will be very expensive to heat. If we were to try and heat this house to 21 degrees C in every room all the time for 6 months of the year it would cost over £3000 a year.

A heat pump would help reduce this cost, but it would still be expensive.

If we were to spend some money insulating the house would this make much of a difference?

If we installed UPVC double glazing, cavity wall insulation and 200mm of loft insulation, the heat load would fall to just over 10kW, that's a reduction of nearly 50%.

MCS Heat loss In accordance with EN12831

ABC HEAT PUMPS
Ground and Air source heat pump design and consultancy services

Results		
Total Heat loss	10317	W
Heated floor area	128.0	m^2
Average W/m²	81	m^2

the design temperatures are set in MCS, this design temperature is altered 0.6C for every 100m above sea level.

Location	
location	London
MCS Ambient temp	-1.8
MCS Ground temp	10.2
height above sea level	30.0
Corrected Amb temp	-2.0
Corrected Gnd temp	10.0

Building Details		U-value	% of total heat
External Wall type	1990- 2000 cavity wall 100mm insulation	0.60	21%
Window type	1990-2010 Double glazed upvc	3.10	18%
Roof / Ceiling type	2000-2010 200mm insulation	0.30	13%
Floor type	pre 1918 wood floor vented	1.75	14%
Ventilation loss	Living rooms/Hallways	1.50	34%

At 10.3 kW you would only need 1 heat pump to heat this house.

Again note how:

2.1kW loss through the walls, 1.9kW through the windows, 1.3kW through the loft, 1.4kW through the floor and 3.5kW

	correct on 5/11/21
Current Heating System	estimated run cost /yr
Natural gas OFGEM	£ 2,028.71
Energy Cost	p/kWhr or litre
Cost of Gas pence per kWhr	6.5
Cost of electricity pence per kWhr	20.3
Cost of oil pence per Litre	58.0
Cost of LPG, pence per litre	68.0

though drafts.

The house is much better insulated, so the run cost will fall, it will be much less expensive to heat. If we were to try and heat this house to 21 degrees C in every room all the time for 6 months of the year it would cost £2000 a year.

A heat pump would help reduce this cost,

New system estimated run cost per Year	
£	1,614.20

You don't have to spend lots of money to insulate your house before a heat pump is installed, but it would be a terrible waste to install a green technology and then waste the heat.

In brief:

In this example, uninsulated we would need 2 heat pumps; this would cost over £20k to install

With the cavity walls, double glazing and loft insulation you would need 1 heat pump, £10-12k

You would also save £800 a year run cost if you only had one heat pump and insulation.

It would be crazy to not insulate first

Cavity wall insulation can be installed for £0 with a grant.

Loft insulation is £400

Double glazing is £10k

40 I don't like cavity wall insulation I'm not having it.

The rules for the government grants are very strict, if there is a

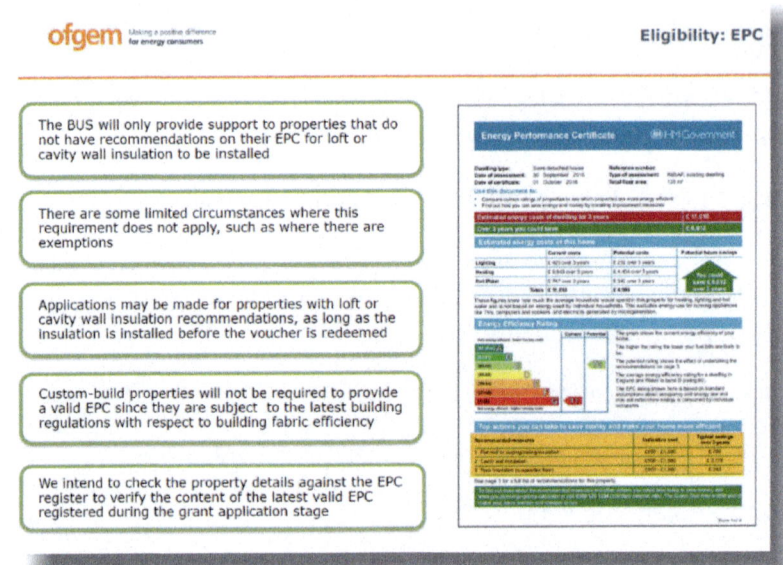

cavity wall it must be filled.

If the wall has not got a cavity or cannot be accessed, you do not have to insulate. There is £5000 of grant to persuade you to get the cavity wall done.

Cavity wall insulation will also save you money on run costs. In the example in Q 40 the cavity wall insulation reduced the heat loss by 3kW.

However you can fill out an exception form called "insulation exemption evidence" if you meet the criteria, you don't have to have cavity wall insulation, if you are not sure Ofgem can help

Telephone: 0300 003 0744 Email: domesticrhi@ofgem.gov.uk

Here are a few examples of exemptions.

Insulation Exemptions

Why is the property exempt?	Which body must confirm this?	What evidence is required?
Due to your property being a listed building	The planning department of your local authority, English Heritage, Historic Scotland or Cadw.	A letter stating that it is not possible to install cavity/loft insulation due to the building being a listed property.
Due to your property being located in a Conservation Area	The planning department of your local authority, English Heritage, Historic Scotland or Cadw.	A letter stating that it is not possible to install cavity/loft insulation due to the building being located in a Conservation Area.
Due to your property housing a protected species that would be materially affected by insulation (most likely - though not necessarily - bats)	Natural England (Bat Conservation Trust), Scottish Natural Heritage, Natural Resources Wales or a chartered ecologist (please find a member of Chartered Institute of Ecology and Environmental Managers - CIEEM website).	You can contact the national bodies for advice, but may need to arrange a site visit and report by a private ecologist. The letter needs to state which protected species is housed at your property and that installing cavity/loft insulation would materially affect the species.
Due to local environmental conditions (e.g. regular exposure to driving rain)	A member of the Royal Institute of Chartered Surveryors (RICS). Please visit the RICS website to find a local chartered surveyor.	You will need to arrange for a chartered surveyor to visit your property and prepare a report. The letter will need to state their RICS membership number.
Due to the structure of your building (e.g. it's a timber framed building)	A member of the Royal Institute of Chartered Surveryors (RICS). Please visit the RICS website to find a local chartered surveyor.	You will need to arrange for a chartered surveyor to visit your property and prepare a report. The letter will need to state their RICS membership number.
Because it would be otherwise unlawful	The planning department of your local authority, English Heritage, Historic Scotland, CADW, or a member of the Royal Institute of Chartered Surveyors (RICS).	The letter will need to state which law prevents the installation of cavity/lof insulation at the property.

41 I only heat 3 rooms of my 9-room house, why can't I have a smaller heat pump?

Our industry (heat pumps) is governed by a standard set out and policed by MCS or the microgeneration certification scheme. The MCS are very clear that we must provide a system to heat the whole house. However, they also say that the calculation must be carried out to BSEN12831 which explains you only have to calculate the heat loss from heated spaces.

This means we can ignore unheated rooms and spaces. I always note these areas in the calculation but do not include them. If a room is not heated by the heating system, we ignore it in the heat loss as it is an unheated space.

Example many people have a porch or utility room or garage which are unheated but are included on the EPC. We can exclude rooms with no heating in them.

If you only want to heat 3 rooms the heat pump could be much smaller than one designed to heat the whole house, but MCS will not allow us to install such a system unless we remove the heat emitters from the un-heated rooms.

What happens when you come to sell the house?

If the house had a such a system what would happen if you tried to heat the whole house?

If you only heat 3 rooms downstairs, do you think it will be warm upstairs?

Try it, turn off the heating upstairs in your house for a couple of days in the Winter and see what happens.

In the 2022 MCS design guide there are slightly revised rules for design temperatures see below:

Space Heating Design Considerations

4.2.1 For systems delivering space heating, the following procedure shall be followed for the correct sizing and selection of a heat pump and related components for each installation:

a) A heat loss calculation should be performed on the building using internal temperatures not less than those specified in Table 1 and external temperatures specified in Table 2 column A or B, according to the MCS Contractor's assessment of the building location. If column B is selected no uplift factor for intermittent heating is required. Heat loss calculation shall in other respects comply with BS EN 12831:2003.

d) Table 1 is reproduced from the UK National Annex to BS EN 12831:2003. Clients should be consulted to establish whether they have any special requirements and the internal design temperatures increased if required.

Room	Internal design temperatures (/oC) from the UK national annex to BS EN 12831:2003
Living room	21
Dining room	21
Bedsitting room	21
Bedroom	18
Hall and landing	18
Kitchen	18
Bathroom	22
Toilet	18

Table 1: Internal design temperatures from the UK annex to BS EN 12831:2003. CIBSE Guide A should be consulted for data for other applications. CIBSE Guide A also contains information on how to adapt this data for non-typical levels of clothing and activity.

We, the heat pump designers are supposed to design you a system to meet these temperatures, but its your house, tell the assessor the temperatures you want the house to be. If they note any variations its still ok.

42 If I have an AGA can I have a heat pump?

AGAs can be fired with wood, gas, LPG or oil. MCS obviously would rather you didn't have this heat source. But you don't have to remove the AGA if you have a heat pump.

If you want the boiler Upgrade Scheme Grant the AGA must not be used to heat the radiators in the house, it must be freestanding. We designers have to calculate everything with the AGA not included and the room its in deleted too. We treat the room with the AGA in it as not a heated room as far as the heat pump is concerned. See previous question. The MCS are worried that they will pay you a grant and then you will use the AGA to heat the house, in effect you get a grant for using fossil fuels.

If your AGA is wood fired it is known as an uncontrolled heat source, i.e you cant turn it on and off easily.

43 If I have storage heaters can I have a heat pump?

Yes.

Storage heaters are 100% electrically powered. There is no boiler and there is no pipework. Once they are removed there is no heating infrastructure in the house at all.

If you want to use a heat pump you need to install pipework, a heat pump, a hot water cylinder and radiators, it can be very expensive. But it's easier for the installers because the whole heating system will be new and of course can be designed to work in perfect harmony with your heat pump.

Storage heaters are generally used because they are cheap to

buy and install but horribly expensive to run.

Storage heaters operate at 100% efficiency, they take electricity and convert it into heat. The idea is brilliant but horribly flawed.

At night when the electricity is cheap the electric heaters warm heavy concrete blocks inside the heaters. The blocks act as heat batteries.

By opening the vents on the heater, you can adjust how quickly the heat leaves the blocks and warms the room. The consumer must judge how long to heat the blocks up and how slowly to release the heat. They are totally dumb machines so don't help at all with this calculation.

Ask anyone who has storage heaters, they are always not warm enough or are only hot for a while, once the heat has left the heaters there is no more available. Their only redeeming feature is they are cheap to buy and install.

Heat pumps use electricity, but they capture free renewable energy from the air outside, you get 3 or more units of heat for every unit of electricity you use. Heat pumps cost less than a third to run compared to storage or any other direct electric heaters.

44 If I rent, who gets the RHI / Boiler upgrade voucher?

The boiler upgrade scheme starts in April 2022.

The way it works is the government give the installer a grant of £5000 when they complete the installation in your house.

The voucher goes to the installer themselves.

The homeowner is the owner of the heating system, they should get £5000 knocked off the installation cost by the installer.

The owner of the heating system is usually the landlord but if you rent, I'm sure the landlord would be happy if you paid to have a heat pump installed. If you, do you benefit from the voucher.

45 What is the return on investment? is it better on oil, lpg or gas

One of the most common concerns with a heat pump is the time it will take to return its costs. It's quite an interesting and odd concept, most things we buy have no return on investment, for example your car, or fridge or TV. But with heating it's a common question.

Although it's a good financial question we should also be asking if the return is long, or infinite are you the consumer willing to make a sacrifice to reduce your carbon impact on the planet? How much is that worth to you?

The calculation is very simple as follows:

We assume that people who are thinking about replacing their boiler with a heat pump are doing so because the boiler needs attention / upgrade. So, there is an assumption that the homeowner would have a quote for replacing the gas boiler. Typically, a gas boiler costs £3-4k to replace

Return on investment calculation:

Cost of heat pump installation – the cost of a new boiler = Heat pump premium.

Heat pump premium - £5000 boiler upgrade voucher = cost to be covered.

Run cost of the boiler – run cost of the heat pump is the annual run cost saving

Cost to be recovered / annual run cost saving is the return on investment in years.

Luckily, we work this out for you using simple tools, here are some examples

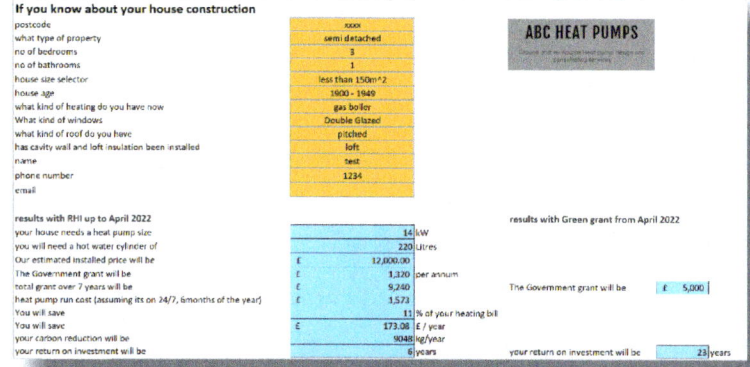

Gas boiler:

Oil boiler

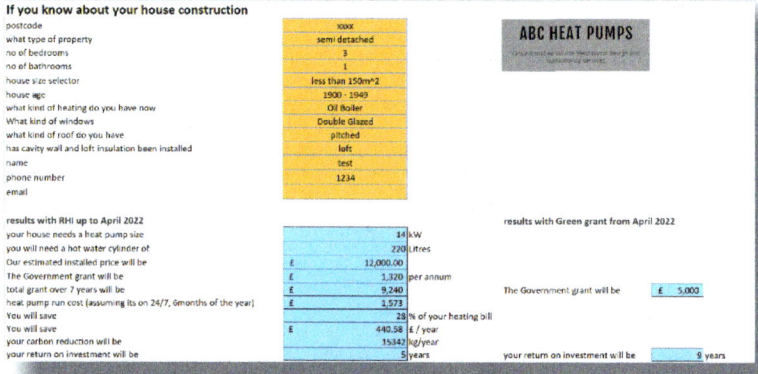

LPG

We use these tools so consumers can decide whether a heat pump is a good choice in the customers property.

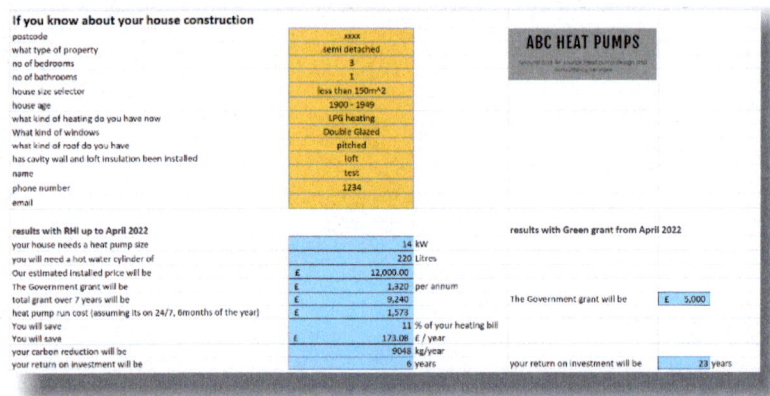

It's very important to make sure any of these tools have current and useful energy prices in them. Any change in the energy price can make some big changes to the return on investment.

46 What is an Agile tariff?

Most people buy their energy at a fixed rate, I pay £0.30 / kWhr all day every day.

You can buy your electricity at a variable rate taking advantage of low-cost periods and turning your demand off when the price rises. This is called an Agile tariff. You are given 24 hours' notice what the price will be tomorrow by the half hour period.

In theory you could set timers on your electrical devices to run in cheap periods and switch off when its expensive.

In practice Agile tariffs are used with batteries so you charge them when they are cheap and use the batteries when electricity is expensive. Going agile without a battery is difficult, do you want to sit in the dark for 30 mins because electricity is expensive?

There are thermostats and apps to control your devices which work really well with Agile tariffs.

The idea of having a variable tariff is that you can either manually or automatically adjust your electricity usage as the price goes up and down. The advantage being that if you use most of your electricity in the cheap periods you will save money. When energy is expensive the heat pump will slow down using the energy stored in the wall's floors and structure of your house to maintain temperature. Most agile variable tariffs let you know what the cost will be up to a day in advance so you can plan.

Ask yourself this:

With agile tariffs the price changes but it's not in your control.

You need your heating system to be able to know when to go flat out and when to work less hard to get the best of these

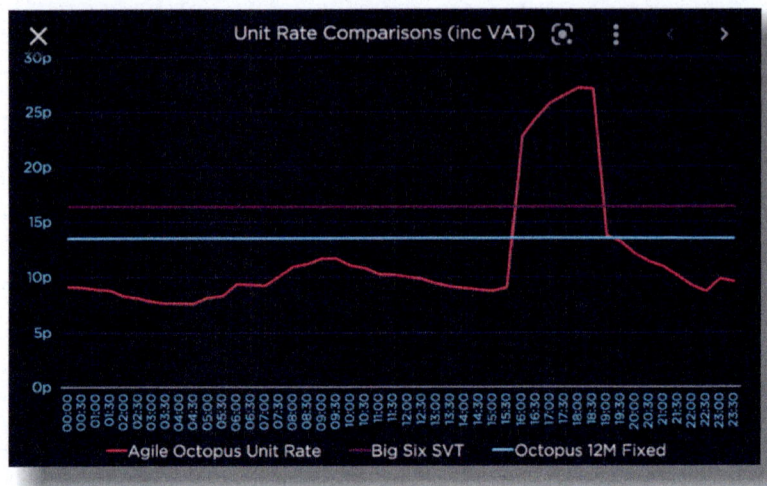

tariffs.

If your house is old and drafty its likely in cold weather that you will want to run the heating pretty much all the time, so it's hard to vary your use with the tariff cost. In newer well insulated properties turning off or down the heating for an hour won't have much impact on the house temperature so it can be very effective.

If its automated this helps a lot, that's where super intelligent thermostats like Homely comes in. Homely knows what the electricity price will be 24 hours in advance, it will work hard when the energy price is low and build the heat and hot water up in your house. Homely also knows, by learning, how quickly your house temperature will change when the heating comes on and off. Homely also speak directly to the unit so they can push the unit to work hard when the electricity is cheap to help your house quickly get back to temperature.

47 Is a heat pump cheaper than a boiler to buy?

Discuss: How much is a heat pump to buy? You can buy a heat pump for as little as £3k.

Do you need any other parts? Yes, heat pumps need parts to connect them to your heating system.

How much is the whole kit? **If you also need a cylinder (you will)**

How much is a boiler?

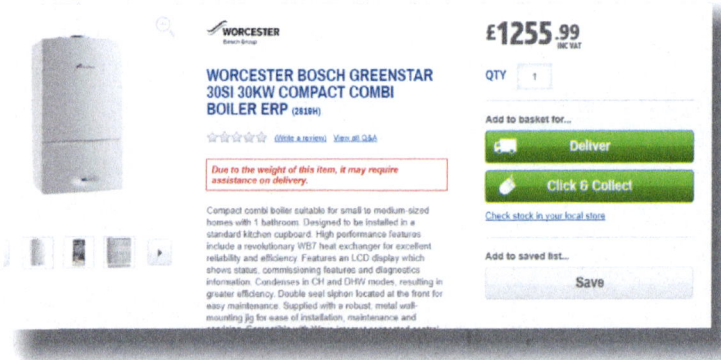

Boilers don't need fitting kits, or if they do, they are very simple and cheap.

Heat pumps are more expensive to buy than boilers.

48 If I live in a huge, old house can I have a heat pump?

Domestic heat pumps are usually available with capacities of up to 16kW. Bigger units are available, but they tend to need 3 phase or commercial power supplies. If you need more than 16kW you have several avenues to explore:

- More than one heat pump
- A heat pump assisted by another heat source, boiler etc
- Another technology, ground source, biomass etc

I have put together a simple matrix below to roughly estimate

heat load calcuator Grid kWs							
year / floor area	100m^2	150m^2	200m^2	250m^2	300m^2	400m^2	500m^2
pre 1918	12000	16500	20000	25000	30000	40000	50000
1918-1970	10000	13500	16000	20000	24000	32000	40000
1970-1990	9300	12000	14200	17750	21300	28400	35500
1990-2000	8400	11250	13000	16250	19700	26000	32500
2000-2010	6000	7500	8800	11000	13200	17600	22000
2010-2016	4600	6000	7200	9000	10800	14400	18000
2016-2020	3600	5250	6600	8250	9900	13200	16500
2016-2020 with HRV	2900	4200	5400	6750	8100	10800	13500

the heat loss of your house. It's for guidance only.

It's possible to heat any size house with a heat pump, but if the house is really large, we start to have problems with available power and deciding where we are going to site the units. We also have to consider that you always need planning permission if you have more than one heat pump.

Dual fuel or Hybrid heating systems are popular in larger properties. We cover these in q 28

49 Can the heat pump just do hot water or

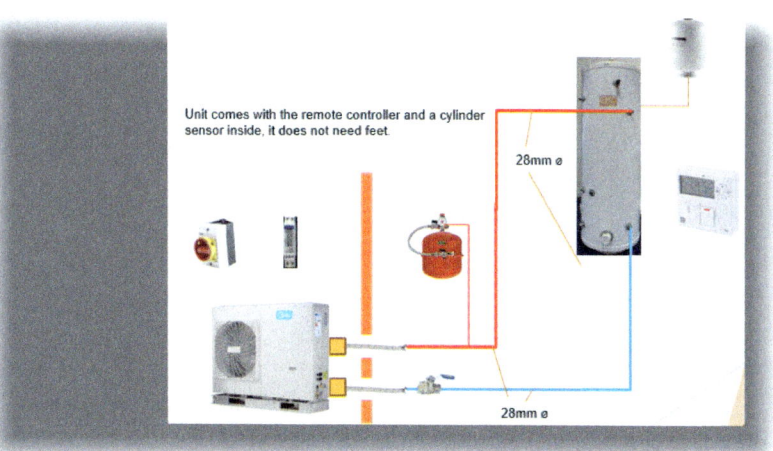

heating; does it have to do both?

Hot water only heat pumps are very simple, the heat pump connects directly to the cylinder. There is no need for any headers or valves or extra pumps. It's a very simple installation. We disable the heating functions at commissioning to stop heating being turned on by mistake.

Heating only heat pumps are also simple, we often use this

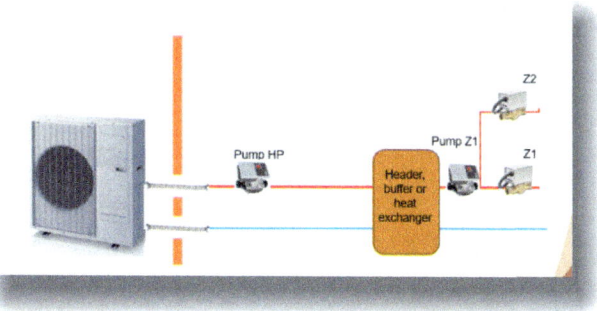

configuration for heating swimming pools.

50 How big is a heat pump and how much space do I need for it?

Heat pumps tend to be made in two model configurations:

Tombstones

And short fat units.

The short fat units are wider and deeper but short, the tombstones are skinnier and taller. The market is moving away from tombstone units now. Short and fat is the new, tall and thin.

When you are planning your installation, you need to know the size to check the unit won't obscure any windows. All heat pumps make a noise so they should be away from bedrooms and neighbours if possible. They like to have their backs against the wall to stop them being blown over.

But the most important thing is to make sure the air does not go through the unit twice. Every time we pass air through the unit, we remove about 10 degrees C from it. We don't want to try to remove another 10 degrees C from the air by passing it through

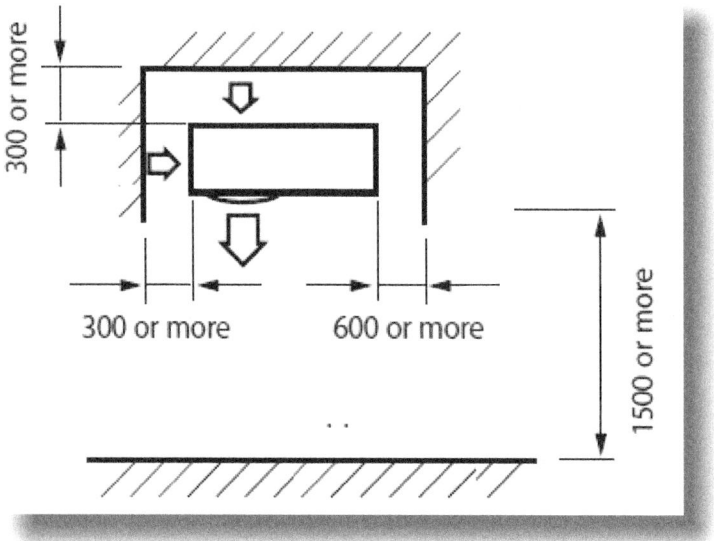

again, if we did, we call this recirculation.

The next consideration is where will all the air from the unit blow?

Manufactures ask for 300mm of clearance at the back to let the air in, 300mm to the right and 600 to the left so we can work on the unit and about 1500mm at the front.

It's important also to allow for drainage, the unit will also pull a bucket full of air out of the air every hour and drop it on the ground through a drain.

THE END

Of part 1

The questions:

1 Why are people talking about heat pumps and what problem do they solve?

2 What is a heat pump?

3 How does a conventional heating system work and what does it look like?

4 How does a heat pump work?

5 Is a heat pump Noisy?

6 Is a heat pump cheaper to run than a boiler?

7 Is a heat pump more efficient than a boiler and what is COP?

8 What temperature does a heat pump or boiler work at and what effect does that have in the house?

9 Do I need special radiators or underfloor heating when using a heat pump? And why are the radiators so big?

10 Can you buy a high temperature heat pump? And is it expensive to run?

11 Do I have to have a hot water cylinder?

12 Why can't I keep my old cylinder?

13 Do heat pumps have to be next to the house or can they go down the garden?

14 Heat pumps are ugly, can I put them inside?

15 Can I put a trellis over it?

16 How long will a boiler or heat pump last?

17 People say heat pumps don't work, is this true?

18 Will heat pumps get more efficient, prettier, or cheaper in the next 5 years?

19 Will I be cold in winter? Heat pumps don't work when it's cold.

20 Will a heat pump work when its cold outside? It was minus 25 C last winter.

21 Will I run out of hot water?

22 What is the carbon saving from a heat pump and what is a carbon footprint?

23 if they run on electricity, how can they be renewable?

25 Can I have a Solar PV diverter, Eddi, Solar I boost and a heat pump?

26 Will a battery power my heat pump?

27 Can I combine my heat pump with a wood burner?

28 Can I combine my heat pump with a boiler? Hybrids explained

29 Can I cool with a heat pump?

30 Am I better waiting for Hydrogen boiler or nuclear fusion?

31 Why isn't there a combi heat pump?

32 Can you use more than one heat pump if the house is big?

33 What is the biggest heat pump you can buy?

34 If heat pumps are expensive can I get a grant?

35 How do I get the BUS Boiler upgrade Scheme voucher / grant?

36 What is an Energy Performance certificate

37 How do I know what heat pump I need at home?

38 Are old houses ok with heat pumps / how old? Isn't new build better?

39 Do I have to modify my house to be heat pump ready? do I have to insulate it?

40 I don't like cavity wall insulation I'm not having it

41 I only heat 3 rooms of my 9-room house, why can't I have a smaller heat pump?

42 If I have an AGA can I have a heat pump?

43 If I have storage heaters can I have a heat pump?

44 If I rent, who gets the RHI / Boiler upgrade voucher?

45 What is the return on investment? is it better on oil, lpg or gas?

46 What is an Agile tariff?

47 Is a heat pump cheaper than a boiler to buy?

48 If I live in a huge, old house can I have a heat pump?

49 Can the heat pump just do hot water or heating; does it have to do both?

50 How big is a heat pump and how much space do I need for it?

About the Author:

Graham Hendra is a heat pump consultant working for ABC heat pumps limited.

He has been working in the renewable heat sector since 2008

He spends his time training, designing systems, writing manuals, and blogging about heat pumps on Linked In.

He feels the subject is not very complicated, it's just badly explained, he hopes this book helps.

Contact Graham on Graham@abcHeatpumps.co.uk

Graham I really like you but I'm not reading that rubbish

Katie Floyd

Friend, Critic and Customer

Printed in Great Britain
by Amazon